SMART PRODUCT DESIGN

SendPoints

SMART PRODUCT DESIGN

© 2017 SendPoints Publishing Co., Ltd.

EDITED & PUBLISHED BY SendPoints Publishing Co., Ltd.

PUBLISHER: Lin Gengli

PUBLISHING DIRECTOR: Lin Shijian

CHIEF EDITOR: Lin Shijian

EXECUTIVE EDITOR: Huang Shaojun

ASSISTANT EDITOR: Luo Yanmei

EXECUTIVE ART EDITOR: Chen Ting

PROOFREADING: Jeff Karon, Huang Shaojun

REGISTERED ADDRESS: Room 15A Block 9 Tsui Chuk Garden, Wong Tai Sin, Kowloon, Hong Kong

TEL: +852-35832323 / **FAX:** +852-35832448

OFFICE ADDRESS: 7F, 9th Anning Street, Jinshazhou, Baiyun District, Guangzhou, China

TEL: +86-20-89095121 / **FAX:** +86-20-89095206

BEIJING OFFICE: Room 107, Floor 1, Xiyingfang Alley, Ande Road, Dongcheng District, Beijing, China

TEL: +86-10-84139071 / **FAX:** +86-10-84139071

SHANGHAI OFFICE: Room 307, Building 1, Hong Qiang Creative Zhabei District, Shanghai, China

TEL: +86-21-63523469 / **FAX:** +86-21-63523469

SALES MANAGER: Sissi

TEL: +86-20-81007895

EMAIL: overseas01@sendpoints.cn

WEBSITE: www.sendpoints.cn / www.spbooks.cn

ISBN 978-988-77572-8-3

CONTENTS

≡ Success Begins and Ends with User Experience

Product design has entered a new and exciting era. The first 30-years of Moore's Law created a technological opportunity for new products that were dominated by engineers. The focus was on function: automation, communication, and convenience in everyday tasks. Products were often boxy and difficult to use for the non-technically savvy. But the last 20 years of higher speed and computation power at ever decreasing cost has enabled product developers to shift their focus from industrial function to user experience and lifestyle. Now the emergence of the Internet of Things (IoT) has made every product multi-functional and multi-experiential. Smart products replace simple mechanical function with adaptive function informed by data from the operational and environmental context. Bicycles are no longer just mechanical implementations of human-powered transportation. Refrigerators no longer just keep food cold, and yoga mats are not just a soft surface upon which to exercise. Today the user is seamlessly connected to their environment and any relevant information to their situation. Every "thing" speaks data and the world streams information to the user to help enhance their experience.

The IoT has disrupted the context of product design, complicating it with connectivity, massive amounts of data, and an immediacy of user expectations. Product designers today have to create smart products that leverage the technology ecosystem and meet ever-changing user expectations throughout the product life cycle. The fundamentals of good design still apply, of course, but the ubiquity of mobile and connected electronic products has added new considerations for good smart product design.

Good smart product design teams engage with new considerations. The first is an awareness of and engagement with the technology and application trends that are so rapidly changing markets. Products are increasingly responsive to user experiences due to the social networking that makes user experiences immediately visible to others around the globe. Digital twins of every machine and even users themselves convert simple monitoring data streams to real-time, actionable diagnostics. The complexity and volume of information streaming to users has created an increasing demand for simplification. Users are drawn to products that provide contextual information, anticipate their needs, and leverage augmented reality to integrate data analytics into real world experiences.

A returning expectation of users is trustworthy and durable design. A new authenticity is demanded of smart products as users move away from the disposable experiences of feature-driven product releases to long-lived products that automatically learn and adapt to both the user and new entrants to the connected ecosystem. Users expect both the experience and the hardware through which they get the experience to last in the way a well-crafted tool or garment delivers lasting satisfaction.

Finally, the new reality for manufacturers is the transformation of B2B (Business-to-Business) value propositions to B2B2C (Business-to-Business-to-Consumer). Established manufacturing companies often struggle with this new understanding of connected product development due to their limited view of applications and the incremental nature of technology change—the unfortunate frog-in-boiling-water metaphor. No longer can one develop products strictly from a technology feature or simple business-efficiency point-of-view. Smart, connected products live in the hands of users, i.e., consumers, who judge every product by how well it enhances their efforts and how well it works compared to their best smart phone experience.

These new considerations of smart products demand a new partnership between designers and engineers. Within the context of these emerging technology trends, the development teams must operate in a tighter, more integrated design-engineering partnership that embraces both the technology and the user. They must diligently practice the fundamentals of effective smart product design:
1. Agree to and focus upon a clear problem statement.
2. Appoint systems leads who understand the importance of design.
3. Work with designers who understand technology.
4. Follow an iterative build-measure-learn process.
5. Simplify for success.

The last point is critical. As the underlying technologies become more complex, users move farther and farther from maintenance and ownership. Arthur C. Clarke said, "Any sufficiently advanced technology is indistinguishable from magic." "Magic" may be difficult today, but the challenge for product developers is to make both using and maintaining the product a seamless experience. Functional fixes, security upgrades, and new interoperability must all be invisible. The teams that practice these fundamentals will stay focused on solving important problems with solutions that users adopt.

The value of adoption cannot be stressed enough because only through product use is data generated, and data is the new currency in the digital business models of the Internet of Things. Smart product design begins with the user and succeeds when that user achieves their goal through product use—over and over again.

Scott A. Nelson

For over 25 years Scott Nelson has led product development and entrepreneurial business growth as both a technology and business leader. Now as CEO/CTO of Reuleaux Technology, Dr. Scott Nelson helps companies across the USA with strategy and new business development leveraging the Internet of Things (IoT). For more information, please refer to https://www.linkedin.com/in/scottanelson17.

☰ Beyond the Object: the Design of Smart Products

Intelligent objects are certainly not a product of the 21st century. Since the introduction of solid state transistors in the 1960s we've been witnessing the "smartifications" of appliances and toys. Moore's law made possible an exponential advancement in electronics, allowing us to manufacture always cheaper and smaller devices. So why has this term become such a trendy topic over the past years? The answer to this question is to be found in tools, rather than technologies. Electronic prototyping platforms such as Arduino and the creation of fablabs and makerspaces, along with the online communities that formed around them, gave design students, garage makers and creatives in general the spaces, equipment and support for testing their ideas. The subsequent rise of interest in smart objects also encouraged manufacturing companies and design studios to take a chance, and invest in the launch of their own product. And with the diffusion of smartphones and an increasingly powerful and social Web, the opportunities for interactive, connected products exploded.

Among the most common smart products available today, many promote the possibility of remote control through a smartphone app as a core feature, but smart products really shine when they thoroughly engage with the online world. Connectivity make things able to access to all sort of data; it allows them to take part in our digital life, integrating with the social networks we use every day; and lastly, it offers devices the possibility to take advantage of a great number of software services. This last aspect in particular is steering the design of smart products in exciting directions. Major technology groups (Google, Microsoft, Amazon) and a number of other start-ups, driven by advancements in machine learning, are providing ready-to-use, state-of-the-art tools such as voice recognition, object recognition, language translation, face analysis and many others. Accessible through Web APIs, those capabilities can expand dramatically what a "thing" can do when connected online, introducing in their behaviors levels of sophistication that were unthinkable a few years ago. Smart products are learning to communicate with humans in their own language, understanding the world they live in and showing a great degree of autonomy.

At my work, we've recently started researching methodologies to design for increasingly complex and nuanced interactions, and the preliminary step was to create a language that allowed us to work in this different scenario. David Rose's idea of Enchanted Objects offers a suitable metaphor when we are limited to augmenting ordinary objects (like his example of an umbrella that lights up when it is about to rain), but it is a short-lived solution when we deal with more complex technologies. To quote Tobias Revell on the subject, "when magic goes wrong, the narrative of magic can quickly turn to horror". With the intent to avoid either of those extremes, we drafted a framework that guided us to design smart objects. What we came up with are three archetypal "personas" for smart devices. Is the product's main function to fulfill a specific goal even against the user's direct control? That is a police object. Do we expect the device to automate as many things as possible, leveraging technology to offer the most seamless type of interactions? We call that a butler. Is the product complementing users' capabilities, working in symbiosis with them, but never imposing a final choice? That is a buddy behavior. By employing human-like characters, hinting at modes of interactions we are already familiar with, our aim is to provide us and the users we design for with a set of metaphors that don't feel deceiving and to reduce friction when they don't behave in perfectly predictable ways.

But interaction design is not the only field that requires our attention. When dealing with connectedness, design choices reach far beyond the physicality of the objects and into our lives, both online and offline. Recent news confirms how important it is to try tackle product design with a more global view. Google's shutdown of smart home hub product Revolv reminds us how slippery the notion of ownership is when connected devices rely on external services to run. And a hacker attack in the USA that employed a network of compromised internet-connected cameras teaches us that security is not a matter to be treated lightly. Finally, as objects are increasingly automated, we need to carefully work to make sure they address diversity in the most appropriate way. Overall, the design of smart products lays at the intersection of a number of different disciplines. UX choices can easily interfere with security, and interaction design decisions might lead to privacy consequences. Ergonomy needs to come together with software and data; business choices have substantial impact on the functioning of a product. Smart objects require us to become what architect and inventor Buckminster Fuller called a Comprehensive Designer, one who would eschew specialization to be able to gain a better perspective of the whole picture, a necessary approach for designing smart products that are both useful and human-centered.

Leonardo Amico

Leonardo Amico is a Creative Technologist at Uniform, where he is involved in the ideation, design and development of digital experiences, with a focus on connected products and interactive installations. He's also an active member of international open-source appliances research platform Hacking Households and part of design fictions duo AM-FL. His work has been exhibited across a number of festivals and museums including V&A in London, Salone del Mobile in Milan, Dutch Design Week in Eindhoven and Adhocracy in Athens.

Smart Home

BéKKU

De: Andy Park, Hyun Jin Kim

BéKKU is a smart thing to seamlessly connect family members between home and work, balancing their home and work responsibilities. It allows family members to connect from wherever they are, to monitor home security through mobile apps when they are at work, and to check status of each family members and personal schedules. BéKKU also comes with other IoT-related features, allowing users to watch videos, take pictures, and more.

MORNING   EVENING   NIGHT

The color palette for the BéKKU interface mimics the natural gradation of sunrises and sunsets, in order to bring the users into a state of comfort when using BéKKU.

What were the main challenges you faced during the development of BéKKU? How did you solve them?

In terms of internal components, there are many things that can easily be installed within this project, such as Samsung's Artik platforms and Ubuntu software. Our core challenge with BéKKU was to naturally integrate its aesthetic and functions into the home environment. Would it be rolling around the house? Attached on to the wall? Will it actually look like a robot? We have designed series of forms for BéKKU and interviewed a variety of homeowners with many different cultures and lifestyles. Through interviews, we have found out that 80% of the home owners we have interviewed have vases or ceramics of some sort in their home. And homeowners felt uncomfortable if they knew something was watching over them. Because of these interviews, we tried to stay out of the plain robotic design and set our design inspiration to be much more like modern ceramics. This way, BéKKU can naturally live within the home environment and users won't feel any pressure that something is watching over them.

BéKKU functions with an accompanying app. How did you make them work seamlessly? Can you share your thoughts on this prevailing method and its development or other potential solutions in the future?

Yes, so people in the house will be using an actual BéKKU product and people away from the house will be using a mobile application to be connected with each other. In order to have the right features within the application that can be connected to BéKKU, we ran a number of scenarios to finalize our decisions on which features can be more seamlessly integrated into the mobile application and how BéKKU will make actions reacting to those inputs from the mobile application. Most likely, people who are using the mobile application are the homeowners who take care of children, elderly, people with disabilities, and many others. We figured that it is necessary to provide features that can literally make BéKKU be that person with the mobile application. For a quick example, I am looking at a screen and I see my mother walk across the kitchen. I see that she has not taken a medicine past an hour of her schedule. I can quickly click on a voice feature and say, "Hi, mom, don't forget to take your medicine." And BéKKU says it with my voice at home. Instead of calling my mom, waiting for her to go and pick up the phone, I can just say, "Don't forget your medicine."

For BéKKU's look, the design duo found inspiration from sculptures and ceramics, and made BéKKU naturally integrated into the user's home environment.

I learn from your site that you have done a great deal of surveying for the project BéKKU. What's the role of this part in your work? Can you share your design approach?

Survey and research played huge role in our project BéKKU. We already knew that there are many working parents today, as well as people who need to take care of their family members. This was necessary research for us to support a reason why BéKKU or products like BéKKU are needed in the household since this is a new/upcoming consumer electronics market that many consumers are not familiar with and rarely thought about for their home. The reason why we decided to upload the research within the portfolio is to let people understand that this is a very common but serious issue that many working people are dealing with.

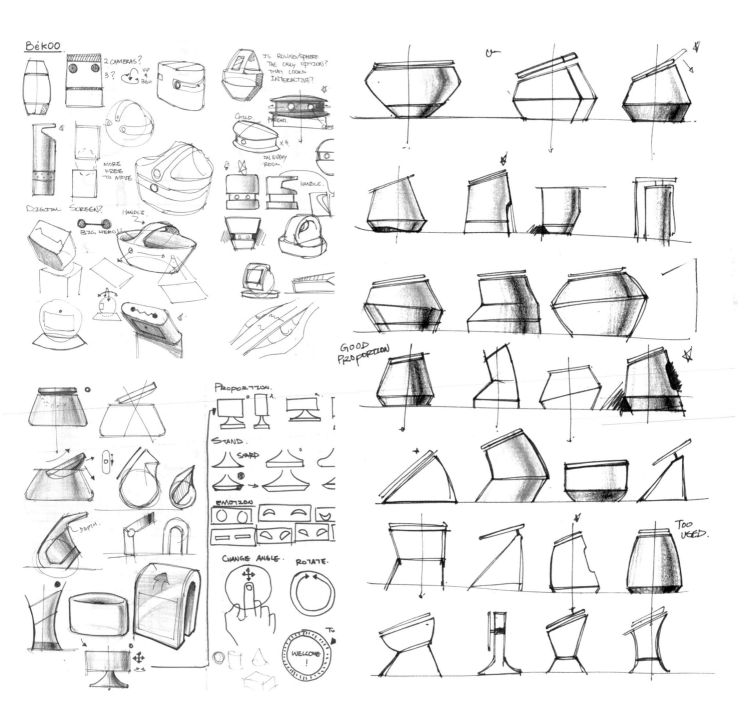

Békoo

2 CAMERAS?
3?
UP
360

IS ROUND/SPHERE THE ONLY OPTION? THAT LOOKS INTERACTIVE?

CHILD PARENT
x4.
IN EVERY ROOM.

HANDLE.

MORE FREE TO MOVE

DIGITAL SCREEN?

HANDLE

BIG HERO!!

PROPORTION.

STAND.

SHARP

EMOTION

CHANGE ANGLE.

ROTATE.

WELCOME !

DEPTH.

GOOD PROPORTION

TOO USED.

⑬

MAIN

ENTERTAINMENT

CONTACT

STATUS

PROFILE

BéKKU INTERFACE

BéKKU has an intuitive interface. What do you think are the most important aspects in making a user-friendly interface?

We came to a point where we had to design the interface and icons that can communicate with three generations, meaning children, parents, and grandparents. In order for everyone to quickly understand what each button does and easily track every page, we used very simple icons and used the grid strictly to design the interface. Simplicity was the key to our goal and it brought us to a user-friendly interface.

The movement of the BéKKU screen was inspired by the sequence of the moon's phases. The platform that the BéKKU screen sits on is bowl-shaped, activating with a lively display. The inclined angle of the activated screen is maximized for comfort when a user is using the BéKKU on tables or surfaces.

On the back of BéKKU, a projector is installed so that users can project the top screen of BéKKU onto a wall or canvas for a wider display.

Privacy and security issues are still people's concerns when referring to smart, connected devices. How does it affect your design and how do you reduce BéKKU users' worries? Can you share your knowledge on the present solutions or technologies that can improve this situation?

This is one of the MANY concerns that consumers have in terms of IoT products. As far as we understand, we believe that private clouding is the most reliable option available for such products like BéKKU since it is not shared with the public but is only accessible by you and the company. After that, it is all about if consumers trust their company's business model of keeping it safe. In terms of design function, when BéKKU is not in use, the screen on the top will go down and display a lock icon so users know that BéKKU is turned off. This may not completely remove the user's concerns, but as far as a design function, it can reduce some of their privacy concerns.

The smart product is a popular concept today, and people rush to make things "smart" and connected. In my opinion, it just makes our lives complicated because not all things need to be smart. What do you think?

I do agree with your opinion. There are many products providing smart features. But sometimes, I feel like the word "smart" is misused in some cases. My definition of "smart" product is a product that allows users to do what they want to do with the product efficiently, rather than letting users know what they need to do to become efficient. Wanting to do and needing to do are quite different.

How do you think smart products will affect our lives?

Not as an industrial designer, but as a consumer myself, I can see people relying most of the time on products rather than themselves. Some may say this is a comfortable and a good thing, but at the same time, some may think it is bad. It is up to individuals on how they feel about it.

Suzy Snooze

Co: BleepBleeps

Tom Evans: Founder of BleepBleeps

Designed based on the concept of "customer need first," Suzy Snooze is a tool suitable from birth and loved by older kids for easier parenting. It is a new breed of baby monitor that actively helps children get to sleep. Her soothing light and sound creates a comfortable and familiar environment for children to sleep faster and more happily. When connecting to the BleepBleeps app, Suzy becomes an audio baby monitor, allowing parents to listen in live to their baby using high definition, secure audio. It also plays music at bedtime, functions as a nightlight with friendly glow, promotes natural sleep hormones and raises its hat to express it's time for children to get up.

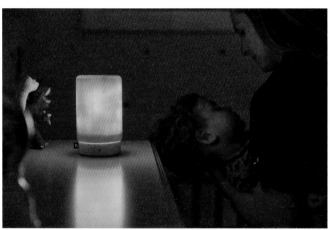
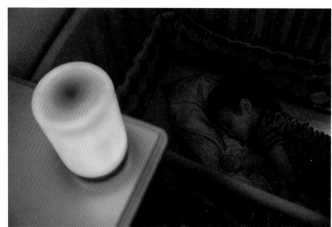

You have various careers. Did they help you to start BleepBleeps?

My background is design, advertising, brand and technology. I've always loved the sweet spot of where design, tech and brand intersect. Then I had kids, the iPhone came out and there was a lot of energy around connected products. BleepBleeps was born!

What were the main challenges you faced when developing Suzy Snooze? Any advice for those at the same stage?

Hardware is hard. And I'm not a product guy. I've had to learn an entirely new industry and teach myself a new career. My advice is to just keep going! Anything worth doing is hard. And we all need to learn how to cope with modern life: finding a higher purpose/calling AND enjoying the everyday struggle.

What were your concerns when it came to the appearance design and material choice for Suzy Snooze?

Like with all BleepBleeps products, we had to find a balance between characterfulness and simplicity. One of the most challenging things was to create Suzy's hat. It needed to be a translucent orange light but also opaque glossy orange plastic when her lights were off. The result is what we want. I particularly like the felt material texture on her base and the way her hat moves on over her eyes when she is snoozing.

Did you ever consider the market factor before beginning this project?

Yes, we talked to many parents and realized sleep is the number one problem for young families. We also worked with leading sleep scientists to make an effective product.

What trends do you see occurring in industry design with the implementation of IoT?

Things are getting smarter. Today's customers (who grew up with a phone in their hand) expect their phone to be the remote control for their life. So many more products are being "connected." It's great!

How do you think smart products will affect our life?

The best definition I've heard so far is: "More things to think about me. Less things for me to think about."

Aurora

Co: Nanoleaf

Inspired by the beauty of the Aurora Borealis, the Nanoleaf Aurora taps into the power of self-expression and creativity through light. The Nanoleaf Aurora is a smart, modular LED lighting system composed of sleek triangular panels. Designed to transform home lighting into a robust sensory experience using wireless voice control, the Aurora panels are outfitted with RGBW color-changing LEDs and can be easily connected together like LEGO. With its easy setup, minimalist form and full in-app customizations, the Aurora frees illumination from the constraints of fixtures. It transforms lighting into a paintbrush users can control with their voice or a finger swipe.

What were the biggest challenges you faced during the development of Aurora? How did you solve them?

We shoot for the moon; it's a part of our DNA. The development of any product will always have its challenges, whether it's making an LED component as reliable as possible or producing an interface with Zen-like simplicity from very complex software code. Working with the right partners and tapping into great talent is always an inspiring part of creating the product as well. We've been selective with integrating only the most cutting-edge, interoperable technologies into the Aurora, which has given us the opportunity to collaborate with experts in many different fields to make our vision for the Aurora a reality.

How did you balance concept expression and market demand?

The Aurora is a result of the market demand for something better than boring old light bulbs. We've had a very strong vision of the solution since the beginning. The Aurora is such a new product; we knew it was important to build something for the people who would truly make this a part of their everyday lives. During the design of the product, we surveyed several thousand people about everything from the finishing details to the functionality of the app. There will always be opinions on the direction of the product, but opinions should be taken in as feedback for improvement. We had to determine whether each component or idea of the product concept was part of the majority or the minority market demand. The final product is a poetic symbiosis of design, customer feedback and strategic market analysis.

There are other smart lighting products on the market. How did you make Nanoleaf AURORA stand out?

Human-centric design. Aurora is a visually stunning product at very first glance. It's a flat, modular, triangular panel with beautiful light output. Its physical appearance hasn't been explored much in the world of design. With the Aurora, light comes from the surface of the product whereas other smart lighting products create color by bouncing light off a secondary surface. Aurora lets you not only create the perfect mood and ambience, but also has the ability to capture emotion. You can create your favorite scenes accurately and vividly, without having to compromise on any part of that personal vision.

It's interesting that Nanoleaf's smart lighting series, such as Aurora with a minimal triangular shape, features geometrical aesthetics. Why this shape?

We wanted the product's shape to be inherently beautiful and universally recognizable. Triangles are one of the most versatile and flexible constructs; it's a shape for the creators and builders of the world. The triangle's modularity is in line with the product's core concept of customizing and creating your own lighting environment. We also wanted this component of building your own light to be as simple and fluid as possible. From a design perspective, it was obvious to us that triangles were the best choice.

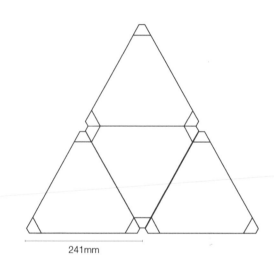

241mm

Nanoleaf AURORA has been developed and used based on IoT. Did any problems arise when you tried to integrate IoT into older systems? Can you talk about your solutions?

The Aurora has been designed as a brand new product that integrates with cutting-edge consumer-based IoT frameworks like Apple HomeKit. The fast-paced nature of the industry has made it challenging in selecting which of the existing IoT standards in the home we should support as a first version, and which we should look to support moving forward. We want to be as interoperable with our products as possible.
We've chosen to integrate technologies that are based on open-source standards from organizations that share our vision of the future—open, cross-compatible, interoperable technology that just works. Regular people don't care about the battles for market share between multinational giants. They just want their tech to work. Our upcoming Nanoleaf Cloud is designed to give our products a stable, central nexus between different IoT technologies to create a seamless user experience.

Today most smart products are controlled by or paired with apps. Can you share your thoughts on this prevailing operating method and its development or other potential solutions in the future?

Humanity is only at the beginning of its journey with technology. Though connected products today are controlled with smartphone apps, future technology will have interfaces that simply disappear into the background of the product experience. Apps are fancy remote controls. Soon, products will operate with minimal human action through insights provided by machine learning and predictive intelligence.
This isn't a future to be feared. We believe that machines should enable the creative mind to create and explore. The Aurora is a connected product that includes advanced control via a smartphone app, voice control (iOS, Google Now, and Amazon Alexa) and a physical remote. It will also be controllable through automation platforms like IFTTT. Giving freedom of choice to the user is at the core of what we believe, because ultimately the Aurora is meant to empower people to create highly personal and intimate lighting experiences that fit into their lives.

What matters most, do you think, when developing smart lighting?

What it boils down to is this: devices that can connect to the Internet will be able to connect to our cloud, which will enable control across all of our products. A seamless experience is the most important aspect of any technology product, and smart lighting is no different. As the name suggests, smart lighting should be smart… and it should also be easy to operate. Everything from the setup of the product to the app should be user-friendly and make the lives of people better. The Aurora lets you personalize your environment with a simple swipe of your finger or with your voice. It's a smart product that instantly lets you make your space *your* space.

Do you have any suggestions for new entrepreneurs in the smart lighting sector?

Ask yourself: what is wrong with today's smart lighting products? You can break this down into two parts: "Smart" and "Lighting." Whatever problems you see in either of these fields that you have an itching desire to solve, that should become your drive and motivation. Don't try to just replicate and outdo existing companies. New entrepreneurs should always be thinking about technology divergence or technology convergence. Envision what's missing from the future today and go make it happen.

Foobot

Co: Airboxlab

Jacques Touillon: Co-founder of Foobot

Foobot is a smart device monitoring indoor air quality. Rather than acting as an air purifier, Foobot tracks the smallest particles in the air, keeps under control all the chemicals generated from our products, appliances and furniture, and sets the right temperature and humidity all day for its users. It also brings the right information at the right time to take care of existing problems and prevent the creation of new ones. With an accompanying app, the monitor provides actionable advice through notifications that become more effective and relevant to improve users' lives.

Why did you develop Foobot?

At that time, I was managing a communication agency focused on environmental issues. I'm a father of 4, and I had my older child who suffered from severe asthma. It was very frustrating not to be able to help him; I was wondering how to fight an invisible enemy. From there came the inspiration to create Foobot. I met Inouk Bourgon, and together we built Foobot to make the invisible indoor pollution a tangible thing. Thanks to its soft-colored lights, everyone at home is aware of the air quality. And now, it allows people to take control over it.

Please briefly introduce the core technology applied to Foobot.

People always think our tech is related to the sensors themselves. Actually, we take the raw data from the sensors and process the signal in a better way than the manufacturer itself does it! After advanced data processing, the second facet of our technology is the cloud our team created to store, process and deliver a very large number of data points efficiently. Big data allows us to constantly improve the accuracy of the information delivered to our users.

What were your concerns when it came to the appearance design and material choice for Foobot?

This had to be appealing and have a strong personality. Existing monitors were not very aesthetically pleasing, and we wanted something different to showcase our technological edge.

Did you ever consider the market factor before beginning this project? How did you balance concept expression and market demand?

We launched the first ever smart indoor air quality monitor, so besides our crowdfunding campaign, there was no way to have a clear market validation regarding our design choice. But the Indiegogo went well, and this was obviously an encouraging signal.

What were the main challenges you faced from concept to prototype? Any advice for those at the same stage?

Because it was such a new product concept, we wanted to share it early on and put something in the hand of consumers that could measure air quality. As we were bootstrapping, we went through a first iteration of the product design in a way that we didn't have to spend money on tooling. We created a design that could be made with standard fablab machines for a reasonable cost and did a batch of 150 of them. That was great because we still had the freedom of radically changing the product after the first feedback (and we did), but the issue of having something which isn't DFM (design for manufacturing) is that partners/clients didn't understand that there was still a significant road ahead to get to mass production, though we are glad to have had a chance to release 2 products instead of one. And now the first design from hardware to software is entirely open-source and available on Github.

Please talk about the aspect of Foobot that you are most proud of.

Being the first to release such a device, of course. We launched in early 2015, and now there are 20 or 30 monitors launched or about to launch. We were a pioneer, and I'm glad that we still keep this strong motivation to innovate. These days, machine learning is what excites me the most.

What trends do you see occurring in the field of industrial design with the implementation of IoT?

Industrial design and UX design are getting more and more related with IoT. A connected product has to have an app and its design becomes part of the industrial design process and ultimately the product experience. On the other hand, some services and startups want to erase the app part, arguing that we can't have an app for each connected product; that it is too many apps and you want things to interact smartly seamlessly. The latter makes sense, but it's not clear that this logic will win. If it was the case, it would remove a big chunk of what is involved in designing an IoT device today.

Currently, there are many networks, standards, and devices being used in the home automation sector. They may be incompatible with each other. Can you talk about your thoughts on this situation?

The impossibility of interoperability and the lack of flexibility are probably why it stayed expensive to automate a home and why it never really took off. But this is only a transition until all components of home automation systems are connected individually to the Internet. APIs are already really common in IoT (Internet of Things) and that's how Foobot interacts with Nest and other connected thermostats.

What do you think are the main challenges and advantages of inventing connected, smart products under the context of Internet of Things?

Security is a challenge in everyone's head in the industry and beyond. At a higher level, to successfully reach a mass market, innovative smart devices must focus on providing tangible added value and not just doing the same thing as before from your smartphone.

How do you see the relationship between humans and technology?

Human's well-being is the end result, and technology should remain a means to add value to people. It's not an end result in itself.

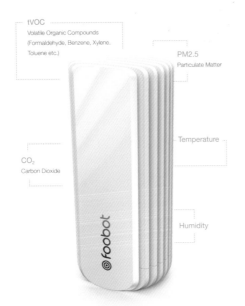

ecobee3

Co & De: ecobee and Lunar Design

Jeff Salazar: VP Design of Lunar Design

Rahul Raj: VP of Ecobee

Ecobee3 is a smart thermostat aiming to reform traditional thermostats that only measure the temperature in one location, often the hallway. The Ecobee3's smart thermostat and remote sensors resolve this fundamental design flaw and deliver comfort in multiple rooms, wherever it matters now. This unique property sets Ecobee apart from others. The Wi-Fi connected system also saves its users an average of 23% on heating and cooling costs. The design vision of "intuitive, clever, and imaginative" makes for a smart thermostat that is both practical and aesthetic.

Why Developed Ecobee3 ?

Rahul Raj: Thermostats—even modern ones—have perpetuated the same design flaw: they only measure temperature in one location, which makes it hard to deliver comfort in other rooms that matter to people. Ecobee worked with the design firm Lunar to solve this problem. The team conducted qualitative research with professional installers and homeowners to understand the ecosystem of selection, purchase, installation, and use. We identified Ecobee's ownable differences and unearthed crucial expectations that would set the Ecobee3 apart. This upfront framing work led to the development of the innovative room sensors, which are wireless devices that measure both temperature and motion that help Ecobee to deliver comfort in the rooms that matter, and not just the hallway where most thermostats live .

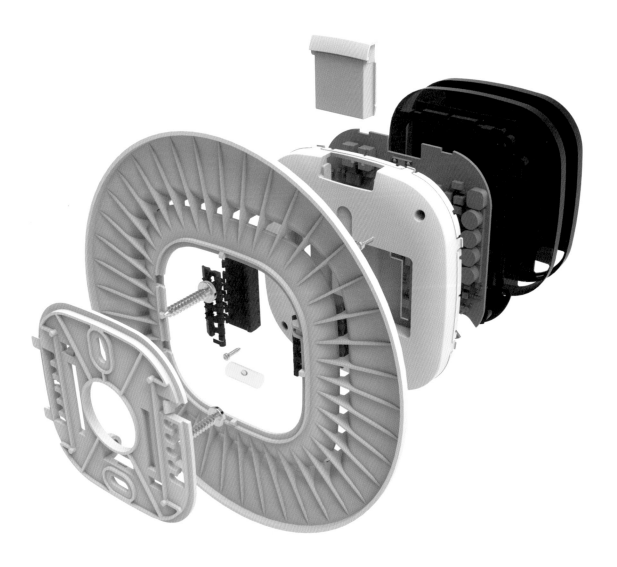

What challenges did you meet when you developed Ecobee3?

Rahul Raj: Achieving a high-quality final product was our ultimate goal, but this was not achieved without challenges during the manufacturing process. For example, both infrared as well as occupancy sensors allow for the Ecobee3 to be smarter, however, finding the perfect materials was a challenge as the different sensors have unique requirements. There will always be small manufacturing challenges to solve, and we continue to seek out better and more integrated solutions with a laser focus on customer experience—all the way from installation to day-to-day use.

What concerned you when it came to materials?

Jeff Salazar: When considering materials used, we placed emphasis on the seamless integration of the screen on the device itself and the crucial connection between the ease of use on the wall versus the app on a smartphone. The mounting plate was intentionally made white so when placed on a wall in either a colorful or more modest interior, it would fit in with the sophisticated design of the thermostat.

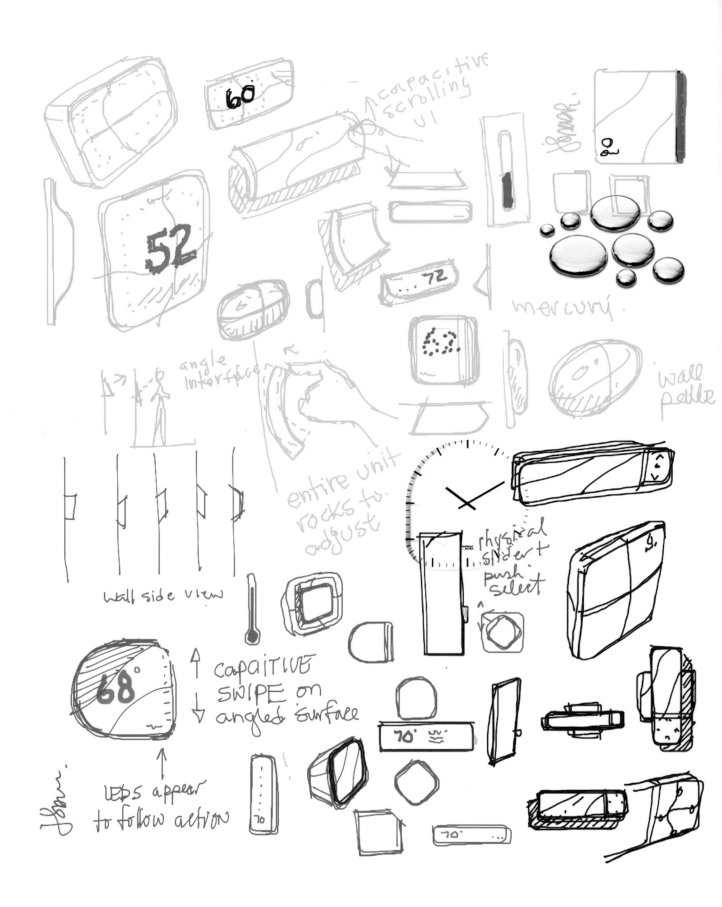

60

capacitive
scrolling
UI

52

72

6.3

mercury.

angle
interface

entire unit
rocks to
adjust

wall
pebble

physical
slider
push
select

wall side view

68°

capaitive
SWIPE on
angled surface

LEDS appear
to follow action

70°

70

70°

What were your concerns when it came to the hardware design of Ecobee3?

Jeff Salazar: The strong contrast of black and white showcases the "smarts," while the soft corners and curvature with friendly UI graphic elements create human design characteristics. One thing customers might not notice with the Ecobee3 is the slight curvature of the touch panel. While most screens are flat, this small curvature also makes the Ecobee3 more human. A large focus for the hardware was placed on improving the install experience of the device, both for contractors as well as the DIY homeowners. The "squircle" shape is an immediately recognizable icon and readily distinguishable. The user interface is tailored to each device, delivering features appropriate for each context.

Why this typeface? How did you optimize the user experience?

Jeff Salazar: For the thermostat's typeface, we used the typeface Gotham in alignment with the Ecobee brand identity at large. In the development of the Ecobee3, it was fundamental to design the digital components in parallel with the physical ones. Through qualitative and quantitative research, we were able to define in detail the appropriate features for each scenario: hanging on the wall, mobile, and PC. Fundamentally, we dug into what our customers want to do in each context and aimed to deliver that experience as simply as possible. It was a big learning experience that not all information needs to live or should be accessed from the thermostat itself.

Niwa ONE

Co: Niwa

Niwa ONE is a solution for people who live in urban areas and want to grow their own produce. Niwa ONE provides a place for plants and automatically takes care of plants, for all of their needs. It will water them, feed them and make sure they have optimal growing conditions 24/7. With Niwa ONE, users don't have to worry about the state of their garden but watch plants thrive.

Why developed Niwa ONE?

I'm from Almeria, Spain, one of the main producers of tomatoes in the world. I discovered many people are trying to grow food themselves for many reasons; one of the main reasons is their concern about the origin of their food. Due to this concern, there is a huge trend towards urban farming, but growing is not that easy. It requires knowledge, time and specific conditions that sometimes are not possible in certain areas such as urban cities. Then I wondered, how can I make the same technology farmers use in my hometown simple and accessible to everyone using technology?

How does Niwa ONE work?

Niwa ONE is a connected software-hardware platform that makes growing easy. Our cloud-based platform automates the entire growing process and runs on different hardware configurations. Niwa ONE is controlled via our mobile app for simplicity and accessibility.

What were the main challenges you faced during the development of Niwa ONE? How did you solve them?

Translating the experience of professional farmers into a smart software is not an easy task, we have spent hundreds of hours learning from them and implementing their knowledge and experience in the Niwa ONE Cloud. The Niwa ONE Cloud is a work in progress and we are working on making Niwa ONE able to learn itself from the experience of thousands of users.

How did you balance concept expression and market demand?

In Niwa ONE we believe in customer development. Customer feedback is at the core of our product development, where we've discovered many different niches where our technology can help different users. That's why we are making an effort in developing a very flexible technology that can be implemented in any size growing system.

Many smart, connected products are controlled by apps. Can you share your thoughts on this prevailing mode and its development in the future?

In the past our devices were controlled with remotes; as our devices perform more complex tasks, richer interfaces were necessary. Remotes or other interfaces are very limited while the now super popular smartphones offer endless possibilities, and furthermore, people are familiar with this interface which softens the learning curve of new technologies. I can see smartphone making the interaction with our smart devices simpler and simpler as they evolve. VR will be a huge step.

Some people enjoy growing plants by themselves and feel relaxed during the process. Niwa ONE may be too automatic for them. What do you think?

That's a really good point. We have users who prefer to be in control of what's happening in their Niwa ONEs while others just want to go autopilot. That's why Niwa ONE has been designed in a way that the user can choose more or less responsibility for their crops, for they can just choose what they want to grow from a list and forget about the rest, just checking their Niwa ONEs from time to time, or they can create custom growing programs for their crops.

How do you think smart products will affect our lives?

The biggest impact to come is the application of big data to our daily lives; now it's just the beginning of all this revolution. Once we learn how to use the massive amounts of data we are collecting, our lives will be more efficient and sustainable. The downside is the risk of our privacy being damaged or even worse, 3rd parties using that data for bad purposes.

What do you think makes a good smart device?

Simplicity of use: many new smart devices are coming down the road and our lives are already complex and busy enough!

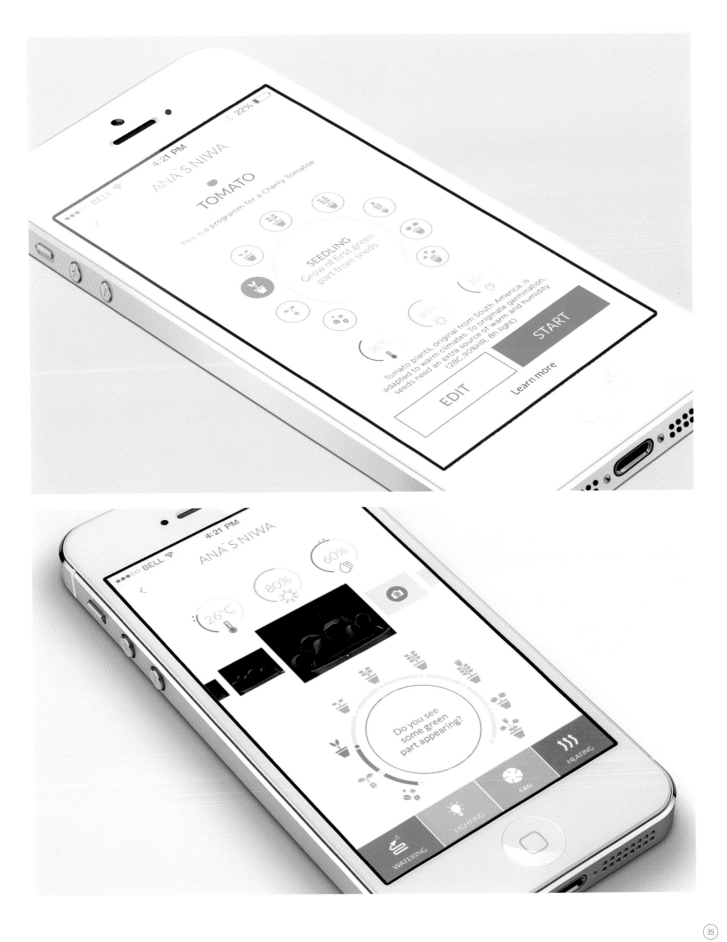

Lyric Speaker

De: Lyric Arts

The Lyric Speaker is the next generation of speakers which display lyrics in sync with the music. When you choose a song on your mobile phone, the lyrics show up on the translucent screen. If it is a mild song like a ballad, the fonts and movements become soft. If it is an energetic song like rock, they become strong and powerful. Music analysis technologies developed by National Institute of Advanced Industrial Science and Technology (AIST) automatically analyze the song's mood and structure, and the built-in expression engine creates motion graphics to each song that's played. Lyric speaker is the world's first speaker equipped with Lyric Sync Technology, which automatically visualizes the lyrics in a beautiful way.

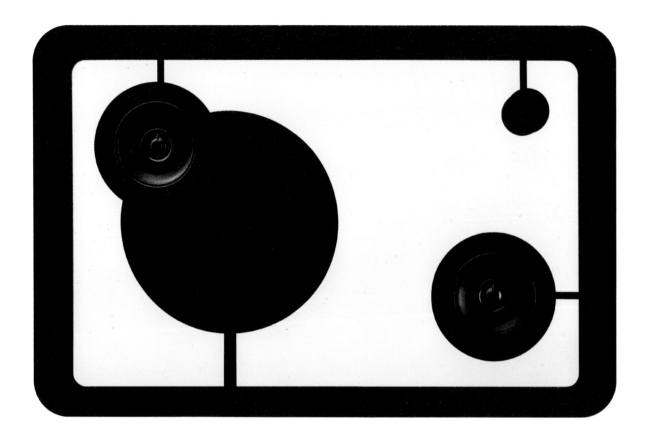

What brought you to the idea of Lyric Speaker?

In my teens, my heart was broken. When I was sad, I listened to Bob Marley's "Get Up, Stand Up" and it cheered me up. The lyrics resonated with me. Have you had this experience? I believe everybody has.

Before the digital age, we listened to music and read the lyrics together. We could experience lyrics more powerfully. However, today in the digital age, the lyrics experience has diminished. We decided to improve music listening by reviving the lyric experience. Our Lyric Speaker is the solution.

Did you ever consider the market factor before beginning this project?

I believe in the opportunity of lyric art. An appetite for a better music experience has always been increasing, especially in the digital era. Accessibility, sound quality… But people leave one thing—the lyrics. Hunger for the lyrics has been increasing after the CD era.

What were your concerns when it came to the appearance design and material choice for Lyric Speaker?

The theme of our team is to visualize the invisible material, "Voice." We use a transparent screen to look like "a floating voice." The position of the speaker unit is designed to concentrate sound and lyrics. You feel like words fly out from the speaker.

What were the main challenges you faced when developing Lyric Speaker?

Our challenge is to enrich the enjoyment of lyrics. We actually listen to the lyrics with our ears, but it is not listened to with the heart. Feeling with our ears and eyes, we can dive into the meaning of the lyrics. It will let you enjoy the world of the musician's heart.

The result is the Speaker powered by Lyric Sync Technology, a speaker displaying motion graphics and offering audio-visual experience. The lyric graphic generating engine lays out the lyric beautifully and draws the graphics in sync with the song. We open Lyric Sync Technology up as an API, so that it can be used in an add-on gadget to your speaker. And it will be used as a built-in module for other speaker makers as well. We aim to make it the next generation standard.

What trends do you see occurring in the field of industrial design with the implementation of IoT?

Every experience will be updated. We will update the experience of music. With our speaker, people can enjoy and understand meaning of the song more, even if the data you play is the same. This speaker enhances the experience of data. Like that, some of IoT will enhance the ability of data. One thing we want to add is that we are not focused on IoT. We just focus on what can drive you to a richer music experience.

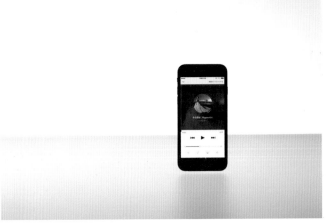

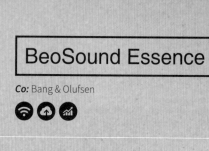

BeoSound Essence

Co: Bang & Olufsen

BeoSound Essence is designed to give people easy access to their favorite music. Without any further device like a smartphone being involved, you just need to connect BeoSound Essence to any Bang & Olufsen active speaker and it starts playing music where you left off last time with just one touch.

The sound system comprises two elements: a hide-away box connecting to the user's music library or streaming services, and a remote, as the system's central control unit. Separated technical functionality gives users freedom to integrate the remote into the living environment.

BANG & OLUFSEN

The design pays homage to classical iconic audio design elements. The volume is set by a big aluminum wheel—a symbol of the audiophile world. The central area of the remote carries Play, Silent, Next and Previous buttons. Through the intuitive array of the buttons, the design team created a minimum appearance for the remote.

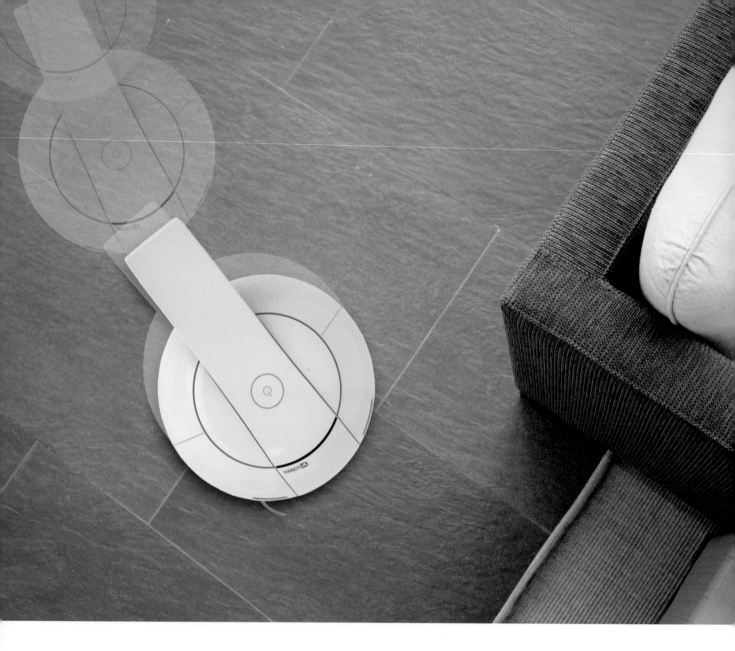

Handy_VA

De: HyeonCheol Lee

Handy_VA is a convertible vacuum cleaner which people can use as both a handheld and robot vacuum cleaner based on their needs. Handy_VA generally operates as many robot vacuum cleaners do. When spot cleaning is necessary, for example, on a sofa, a button can be pushed to release the handy element. Handy and robot vacuum cleaner share a vacuuming structure and filter. When the handy cleaner is attached, the hinged part is opened and the dust in handy cleaner transits to the robot cleaner.

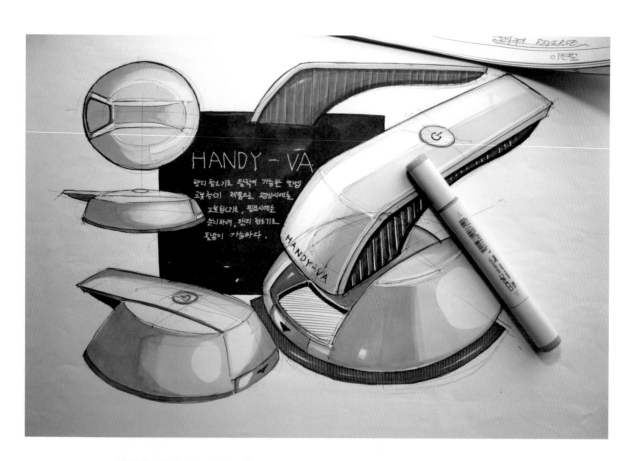

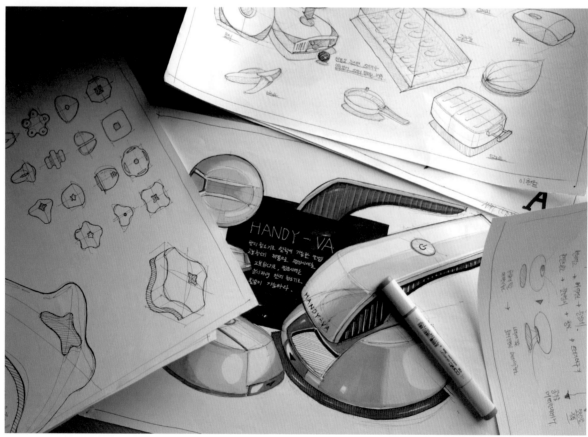

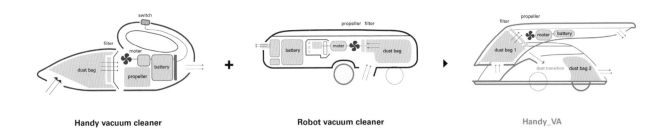

Handy vacuum cleaner　　　　**Robot vacuum cleaner**　　　　Handy_VA

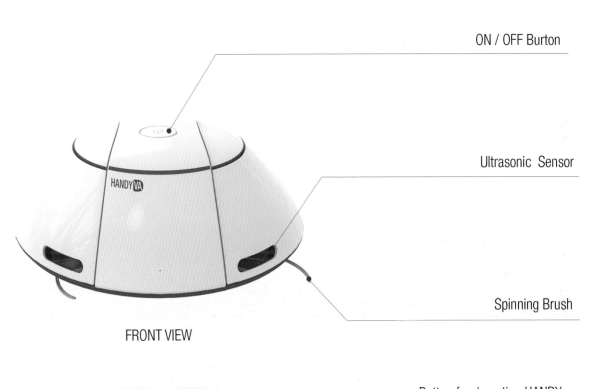

ON / OFF Burton

Ultrasonic Sensor

Spinning Brush

FRONT VIEW

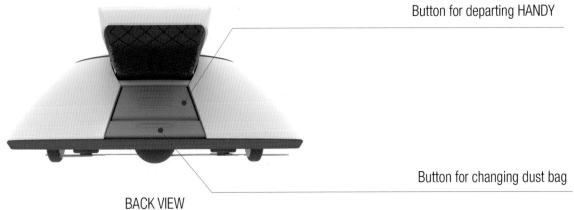

Button for departing HANDY

Button for changing dust bag

BACK VIEW

Notion

Co: Notion

Notion's single sensor makes it easy to monitor your entire home, no matter where you are. It can be used for various purposes. No matter whether you want to know if you left with the light on, or if your water heater is leaking, or if your window breaks, or what the temperature of a specific zone in your house is, you can attach Notion to the object you want to monitor and check its status via the Notion app. Notion allows you to connect to everything in your home with one simple app. Installing Notion is easy: plug in the bridge, place the sensors, and connect to Wi-Fi. And then you can see statuses, change settings, and receive updates.

Boon is an aroma humidifier for office workers to decrease their stress levels. The device syncs with smartphone for power, scent, and sharing controls. Users can easily customize their favorite scent and save those recipes through an available app. They can also remotely turn on their device with smartphones before arriving at their workplace and enjoy the scent as soon as entering their space. A separate water container is designed and equipped to enable Boon to diffuse aromatic oil. From its top, users can simply refill Boon with water.

De: Andy Park, Daniel Kim

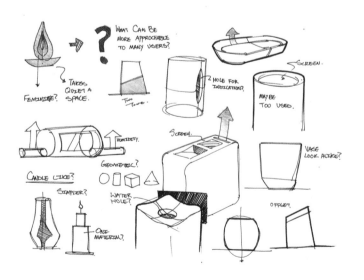

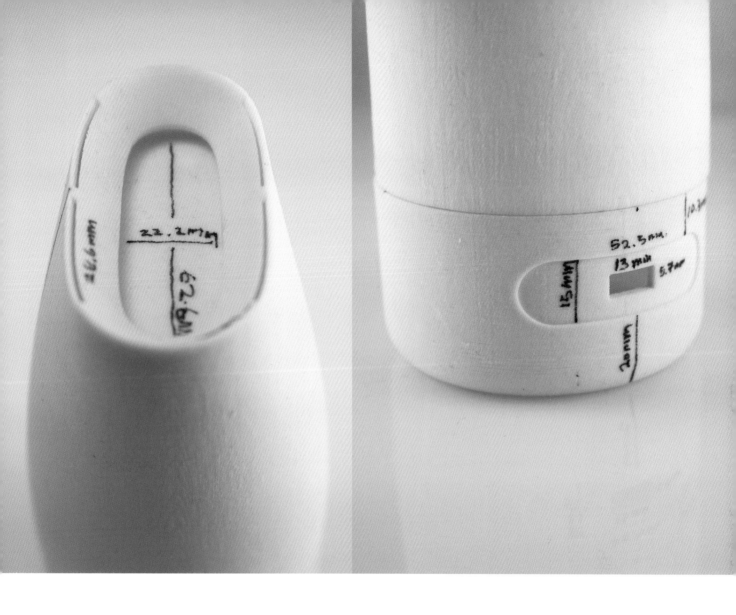

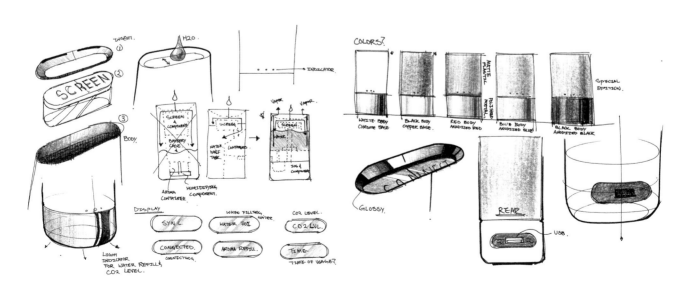

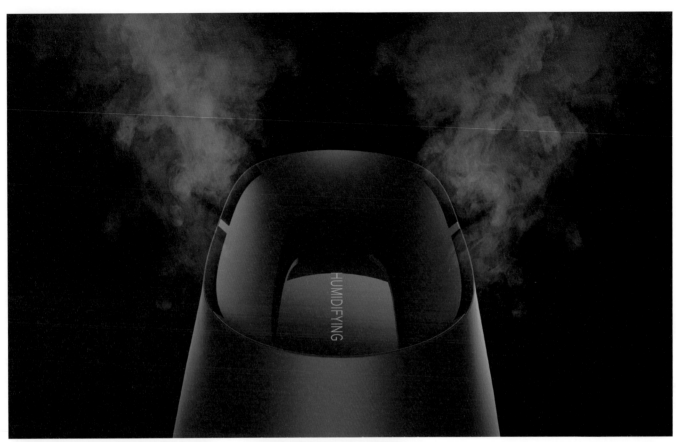

HUMIDIFYING

Netatmo Smart Home Devices

Co: Netatmo

Netatmo, a revolutionary smart home company, has infused intelligence into a series of intuitive and beautifully-designed connected devices—Presence, Welcome, the Weather Station, and the Netatmo Thermostat—which aim to provide a seamless experience that helps users create a safer, healthier and more comfortable home.

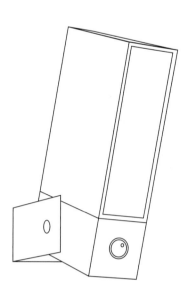

Presence

Presence is an outdoor security camera that can recognize people, cars and animals. Presence detects and reports in real time if someone loiters around your home, a car enters your driveway or your pet is in the yard.

Welcome

Welcome is an indoor security camera with face recognition technology, which enables the camera to recognize your beloved family members when they pass in front of it and notifies you via your smartphone. You will be also alerted if it sees a stranger.

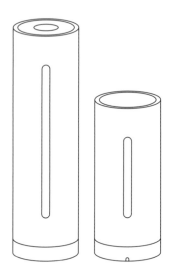

Weather Station

The Weather Station's Indoor Module measures your indoor comfort by providing such vital information as temperature, humidity and CO_2 level, alerting you when you need to air out your home to bring down its pollution levels. Its Outdoor Module provides real-time weather information. The device's app allows you to view your data in graph form for real-time tracking of your environment, observe the cycles and forecast variations around you.

Netatmo Thermostat

The Netatmo Thermostat is designed to save energy consumption and reduce your carbon footprint. It not only allows users to control heating wherever they are, but also lets them schedule heating based on their habits and lifestyle and use the heating only when they need it, thus saving energy.

Dojo

De: NewDealDesign

Dojo is a pebble-shaped device for detecting intrusions and preventing attacks through machine learning and behavior tracking. Once connected to the home network, it adds each device and monitors their activities, alerting you only when you need to take action, and automatically blocking any attacks. Dojo consists of a sleek pebble in a dock. The pebble is free to move about the house while the dock can be tucked away with the router. Light rings on the pebble glow when there is activity on your network. And Dojo's app syncs with the pebble, sending you messages when there is anything abnormal.

Awair

Co: Awair

Awair is a smart home device that tracks toxins and chemicals in your air and gives you recommendations to help keep your indoor environment safe and healthy. Awair's sensors identify five key factors that determine air quality: temperature, humidity, CO_2, chemicals and dust. And the data will be analyzed via the Awair app which then tells you the air quality by the Awair Score and colored index.

Awair offers various modes to help you sleep better, control your allergies, increase productivity, or improve your general health, and also provides personalized actionable insights and quick fix tips that help you develop daily healthy habits.

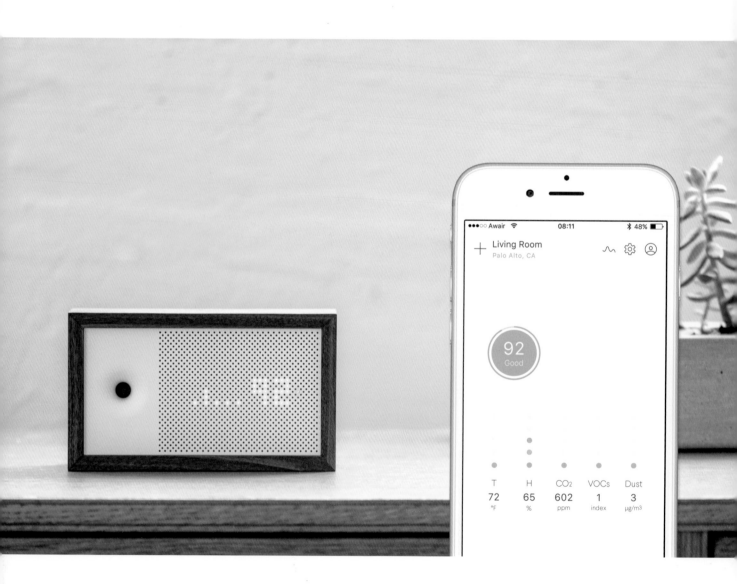

Eve

Co: elgato

Eve is a smart home system for your smart living. The system comprises seven devices, including Eve Door & Window, Eve Motion, Eve Light Switch, Eve Energy, Eve Room, Eve Thermo and Eve Weather, each of which comes with a synchronized app. The Eve family of HomeKit accessories gathers data on air quality, motion, temperature, humidity, air pressure, energy consumption and more. Using the Eve apps, you'll view all collected data and gain insights that help your comfort and make your home a smarter place. Here four of the devices are introduced.

Eve Door & Window

Eve Door & Window functions as a guard for your house. It will tell you whether your door or window is open or closed. Via the device's accompanying app, you can also see the current open/closed state at a glance and view statistics on time and duration to make smarter choices.

Eve Energy

Eve Energy is a smart device allowing you to understand your energy consumption. Through the Eve Energy app, you'll see how much energy your devices are using and turn them on or off with a simple tap or using Siri.

Eve Thermo

With a simple tap or using Siri, you can set a perfect comfort level, or create schedules to automatically heat your home to match your daily routine. Eve Thermo connects directly to your iPhone or iPad using Bluetooth Smart technology, without requiring a hub, gateway or bridge.

Eve Weather

Eve Weather is a smart device for you to know more about the place you care about most. It tells you temperature, humidity, and air pressure. You can simply access your personal weather data at your actual home, right on your iPhone and iPad. Eve Weather is powered by long-lasting, replaceable batteries, so you don't even have to deal with power cords.

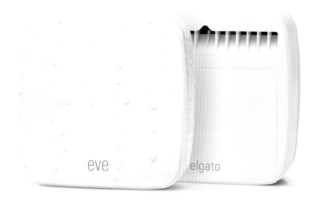

Smart Radiator Valves

Co: Netatmo

These Smart Radiator Valves incorporate three main functions for a smart life and saving energy. The valves detect when a window is open and immediately stop heating the room so as not to waste energy. They precisely analyze external elements in real time—the weather, insulation of the house, the number of people in the room, electrical appliances being used—and adjust the heating of the room to save energy. Users can also manually adjust room temperature from their mobile devices.

The valves feature translucent e-paper screens for a clear temperature display and low energy consumption. Their minimalist design intertwines elegance and functionality.

Co: EasyGo

i-Lit is a cute, versatile lighting device. It has a unique, beautiful appearance but also incorporates a variety of practical and interesting features. With its candle light simulation function, i-Lit brings you some inner peace and wisdom. With high quality RGB light beads, i-Lit is able to adjust 256 colors for different atmospheres. It has an independent speaker cavity, resonance membrane, photomask, fountain disc, counterweight ring, and sound diffusion net. Each detail is weighed and tested to create a perfect performance.

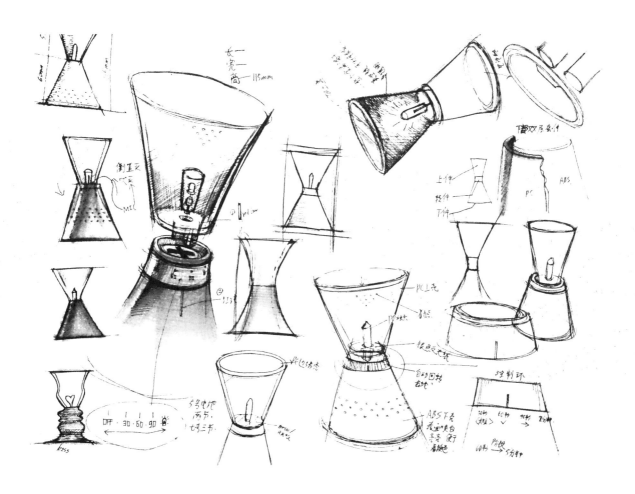

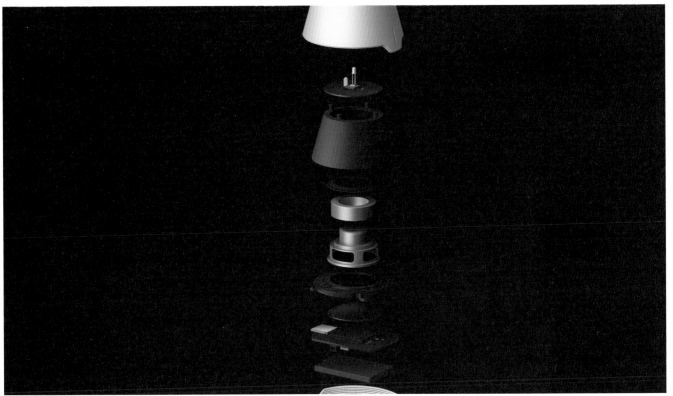

LI-POL
1000mAh

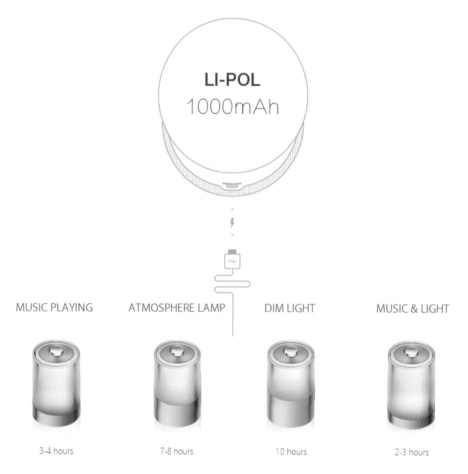

MUSIC PLAYING	ATMOSPHERE LAMP	DIM LIGHT	MUSIC & LIGHT
3-4 hours	7-8 hours	10 hours	2-3 hours

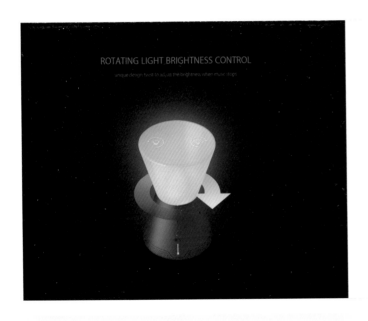

ROTATING LIGHT BRIGHTNESS CONTROL

unique design twist to adjust the brightness when music stops

TWIST TO ADJUST THE VOLUME

twist to adjust the volume when music stops

RGB Led	Candlelight	Music	Music to push	Phone	Time
adjustable lighting adjustable colors	flickering simulation	lights flickering with music wake up flickering	built-in memory play bluetooth speaker	hands free phone calls	time set yearly calender

Touch button	Battery	App
touch button control rotation control	1000+mAh polymer batteries	for iOS

1. Start the APP
2. Turn on the candle blow mode
3. Candle can be blown out via the microphone on i-lit or on your phone

DOTS | Intelligent Luminaire

De: Joaquín Alverde

Dots is a modular luminaire controlled by an app and can be placed in different environments for better lighting. Each module of the luminaire is equipped with a double-sided LED board so the light can go out from both sides. And different modules interconnect to each other with a rotatory axis, giving each piece a certain freedom to rotate. Users can control the intensity and rotation of the lighting device to achieve a desirable temperature and position of each "Dot" via the app.

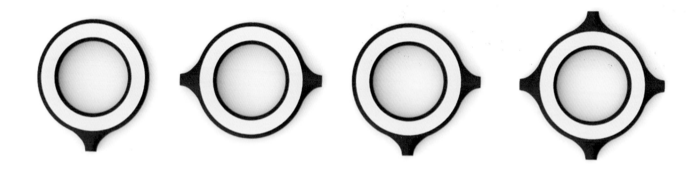

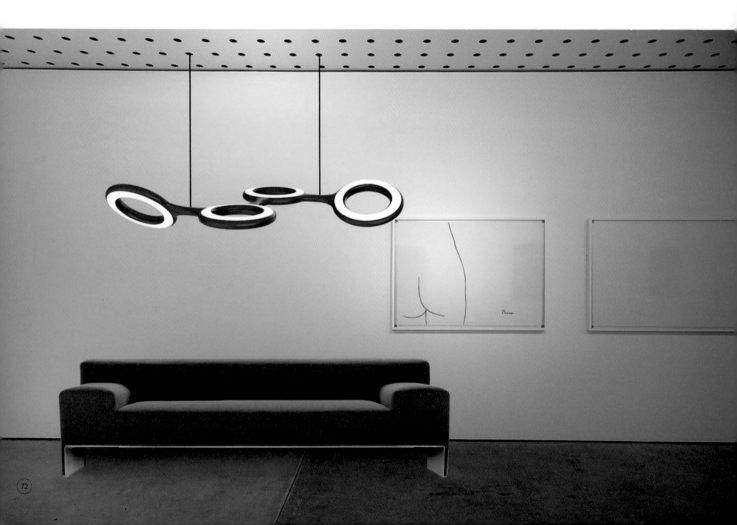

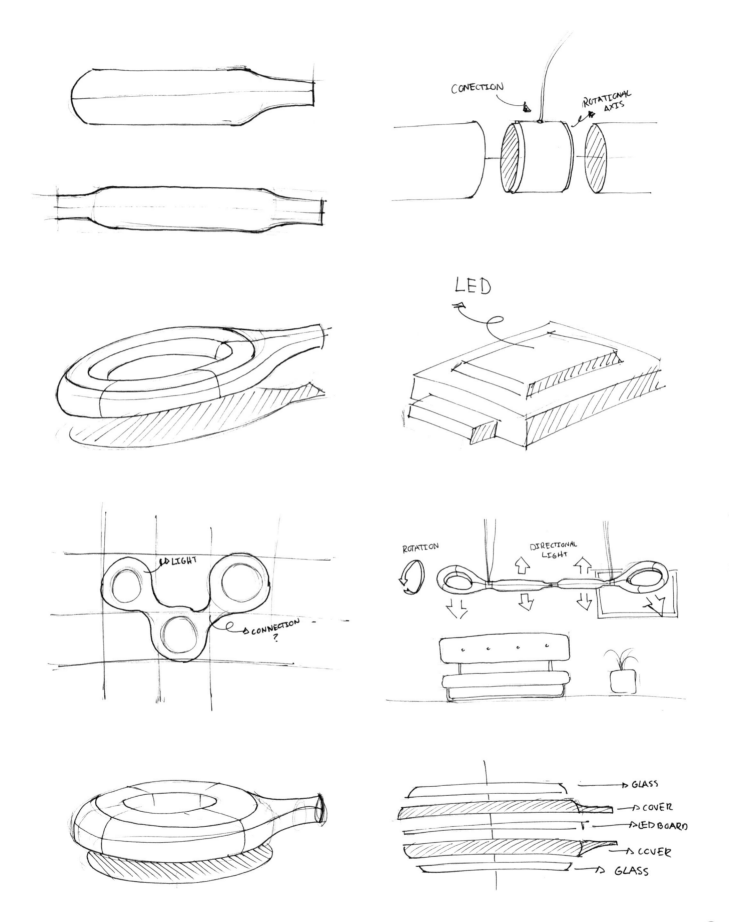

CONECTION

ROTATIONAL AXIS

LED

LIGHT

CONNECTION ?

ROTATION

DIRECTIONAL LIGHT

GLASS
COVER
LED BOARD
COVER
GLASS

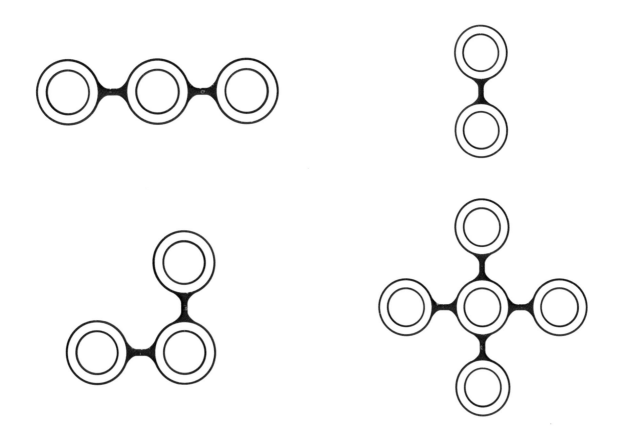

Avea

Co: Elgato

Avea is an app-enabled device to provide perfect lighting for your mood. With Avea, you can fill your house with beautiful, dynamic light and unwind in one of the carefully crafted settings. Set your alarm using the built-in wake-up light scene after a relaxing evening.

You'll get up with a natural sunrise, right in your bedroom.

Avea connects directly to an iPhone, iPad or Android phone using Bluetooth smart technology. Once you have chosen a light scene, the smart LED light bulb will take care of the rest, not requiring a constant connection to your mobile devices. And if you connect more than one Avea, they will automatically coordinate their lighting to create a more immersive atmosphere.

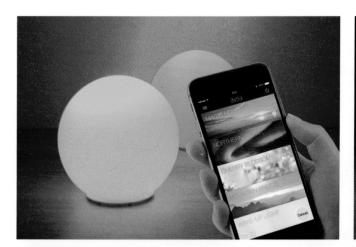

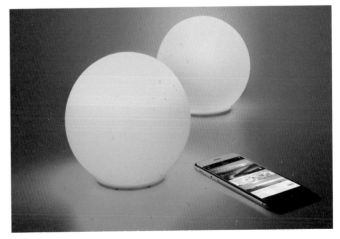

Nanoleaf Ivy Smarter Kit

Co: Nanoleaf

The Nanoleaf Ivy Smarter Kit composed of the Nanoleaf Hub and the Smart Ivy light bulbs is a lighting system featuring strong geometric aesthetics. The Hub takes on a daring dodecahedron silhouette; instead of indecipherable blinking lights, the hub has a string of indicator lights that glow in a geometric shape for a brilliant optical effect that is both functional and beautiful to look at. The bulb impresses people with its premium matte black finish and signature geometric design. The lighting system is voice-controlled and app-enabled, which means you can turn the lighting on or off, or create your preferred ambience by a few words or via your mobile devices.

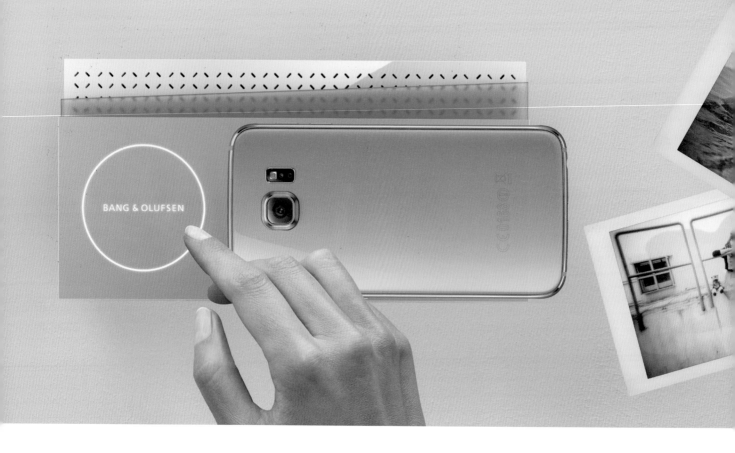

BeoLife

De: Andy Park

BeoLife is an experimental portable speaker from Bang & Olufsen (B&O) to provide users with a rich sound experience while allowing them to connect with family and friends. By swiping an image from your mobile device or by scanning original photos to BeoLife, it generates a list of songs that matches the mood. BeoLife analyses color, facial expression, and gestures to match the mood of the scanned image as close as possible.

With consistency in B&O Danish design language, BeoLife features a modern and architectural form with a plastic molded body and an aluminum top. The frosted acrylic balances out the overall look.

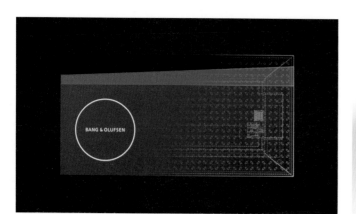 

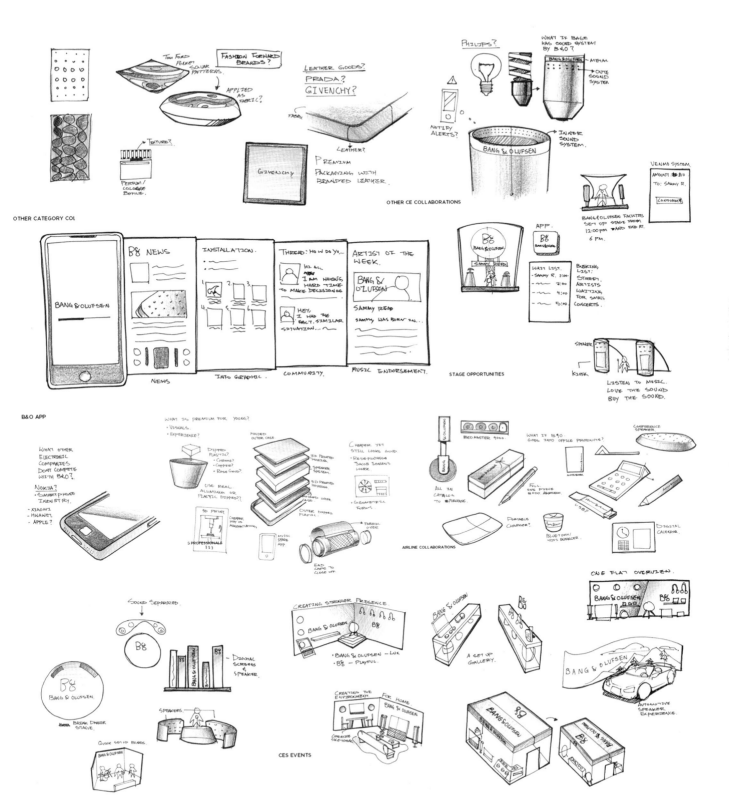

OTHER CATEGORY COL

OTHER CE COLLABORATIONS

FASHION FORWARD BRANDS?

TOM FORD POLKA? SQUARE PATTERNS?

APPLIED AS FABRIC?

TEXTURES?

PERFUM / COLOGNE BOTTLE.

LEATHER GOODS?
PRADA?
GIVENCHY?

FABRIC?

LEATHER?

GIVENCHY

PREMIUM PACKAGING WITH BRANDED LEATHER.

PHILIPS?

WHAT IF BAGS HAS SOUND SYSTEM BY B&O?

METAL

OUTER SOUND SYSTEM.

NOTIFY ALERTS?

BANG & OLUFSEN

INNER SOUND SYSTEM.

VENMO SYSTEM
AMOUNT: $10
TO: SAMMY R.
CONSUME

BANG & OLUFSEN FACILITIES SET UP STAGE PERFORM 12:00 PM AND END AT 6 PM.

B8 NEWS

INSTALLATION.

THREAD: HOW DO YO...
HI ALL
I AM HAVING HARD TIME TO MAKE DECISIONS.

HEY, I HAD THE EXACT SIMILAR SITUATION...

ARTIST OF THE WEEK.
BANG & OLUFSEN
SAMMY READ
SAMMY WAS BORN IN...

BANG & OLUFSEN

NEWS

INFO GRAPHIC.

COMMUNITY.

MUSIC ENDORSEMENT.

STAGE OPPORTUNITIES

APP.

WAIT LIST:
- SAMMY R. 2:00
- 2:00
- 4:00
- 5:00

BUSKING LIST:
STREET ARTISTS WAITING FOR SMALL CONCERTS.

SPEAKER

KIOSK.

LISTEN TO MUSIC. LOVE THE SOUND BUY THE SOUND.

B&O APP

WHAT OTHER ELECTRONIC COMPANIES DONT COMPETE WITH B&O?

NOKIA?
- SMARTPHONE INDUSTRY.
- XIAOMI
- HUAWEI
- APPLE?

WHAT IS PREMIUM FOR YOUNG?
- VISUALS.
- EXPERIENCE?

DIPPED PLASTIC?
- CHROME?
- COPPER?
- ROSE GOLD?

USE REAL ALUMINUM OR PLASTIC DIPPED??

3D PRINT
CHEAPER WAY OF MANUFACTURING

5 PROFESSIONALS

MUSIC SHARE APP

MOLDED OUTER CASE

3D PRINTED INTERIOR.

SPEAKER SYSTEM.

3D PRINTED INTERIOR.

MOLDED OUTER CASE

OUTER DIPPED PLASTIC.

EAR CAPS TO CLOSE UP.

CHEAPER YET STILL LOOKS GOOD?
- REDESIGNING JACOB SENSENS LOGER.

GEOMETRIC FORMS

BED MASTER 9000

FAMILIAR OVER

ALL IN CATALOG TO PURCHASE.

WHAT IF B&O GOES INTO OFFICE PRODUCTS?

NOTEBOOK

FULL ONE PIECE BODY ALUMINUM.

PORTABLE CHARGER?

BLUETOOTH / WIFI ENHANCER.

CONFERENCE SPEAKER

DIGITAL CALENDAR.

AIRLINE COLLABORATIONS

SOUND SEPARATED.

B8

DIGITAL SCREENS & SPEAKER.

B8 BANG & OLUFSEN.

BREAK DINNER STAGE.

QUICK SETUP BOARDS.

SPEAKERS

CREATING STRONGER PRESENCE
BANG & OLUFSEN
B8
- BANG & OLUFSEN — LUX
- B8 — PLAYFUL.

A SET UP GALLERY.

CREATING THE ENVIRONMENT.
FOR HOME
BANG & OLUFSEN

CREATING SKETCHES.

BANG & OLUFSEN

B8

ONE FLAT OVERVIEW.
BANG & OLUFSEN

BANG & OLUFSEN

AUTOMOTIVE SPEAKER EXPERIENCE.

CES EVENTS

The BeoLife app allows users to share memoir with people who are close to them but from afar physically. Interface colors were inspired by the environment with which B&O uses in their commercials, which are more familiar to B&O users.

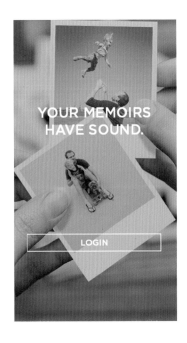

1. Login

2. Main categories

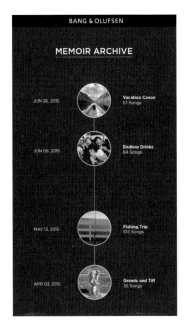

3. Memoir Timeline

4. List of songs for a memoir

5. Play music and share

Cubic: the AI Butler

De: ObjectLab

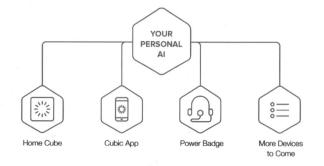

YOUR PERSONAL AI

Home Cube Cubic App Power Badge More Devices to Come

Cubic is an ecosystem enabling you to control your devices, apps, and services from anywhere by simply speaking with it. With Cubic, you can harness the power of all of the scattered technology from anywhere. The services are realized by using two devices: the home Cubic and Cubic PowerBadge that you can take with you anywhere. If you're at work, Cubic can adjust the temperature in your home, turn off your lights, lock your doors, set your alarm, and more. On the go, Cubic can remind you where you parked, tell you how many calories you've burned, etc. In the car, Cubic can give you traffic updates and read you emails and messages. At home, Cubic can tell you when your favorite show is on, play music, order delivery, read instructions while you cook, turn off your alarm, and so on.

Lift-Bit

De: Carlo Ratti Associati

Lift-Bit is a smart sofa that can be controlled with your smartphone. The sofa is made up of a number of modular sections which can be moved around to create different seating positions. Each of the individual stools that make up the sofa embeds a liner actuator which allows them to be raised and lowered. Each element of the module can be controlled via tablet as well as through a touchless hand gesture. A proximity capacity-based sensor detects a hand hovering above at different heights, and permits the change of the height from 48 to 78 cm. Lift-Bit's app includes a number of predetermined shapes and a tool allowing the owner to create new combinations. When nobody is using or moving the chairs, the seating system will get bored and start to move on its own.

Tado° Smart AC Control

Co: Tado°

With a Smart AC Control, Tado° makes any air conditioner smart. Tado° works by using the smartphone's location of its users to automatically adapt their air conditioner to their behavior. When the geo-aware app senses that people leave their house, it turns off the AC; when it senses the approaching of its owner, it pre-cools their place. With the Tado° app, users always know the temperature at home and can change the settings.

The smart control easily blends into the ambience of users' homes with its sleek and elegant look, while offering a matrix LED display and capacitive touch interface for quick and easy manual adjustments. The device is compatible with split (wall-mounted), in-window, or portable AC units and easy to set up. It connects to the air conditioner via infrared (IR) and links to the internet using Wi-Fi—no additional cabling needed.

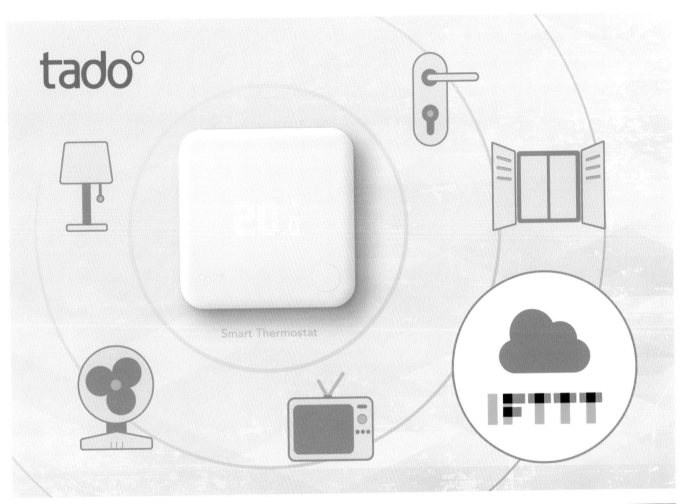

Smart Thermostat

Tom

AirVisual Node

Co: AirVisual

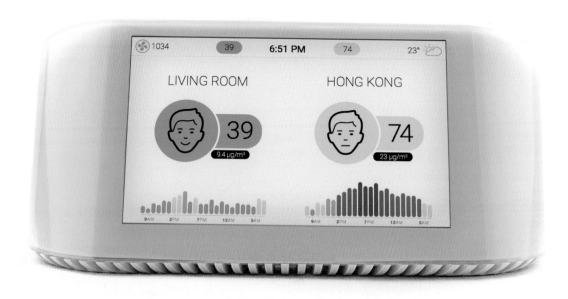

AirVisual Node is a smart air quality monitor helping you track, foresee, and take action against invisible threats in the air. The Node help users to: 1) discover pollution sources in their homes; 2) identify simple actions to improve indoor air quality; 3) monitor outdoor air quality in real time.

To achieve these features, the Node uses cutting-edge laser technology to count particles in the air. Auto-calibration components, instantly considering factors like temperature and humidity, are used to deliver a precise, low-cost air monitor. To enhance preciseness, the Node adopts a downward sloping ellipse to allow maxim air flow between its inside sensors, which contributes to a slim and sleek appearance as well. Moreover, thin blades on the interior allow air into the device from the bottom outer edges, up through the Node, and out the top. The Node's translucent white speaks to pure, clean air and helps the device achieve a universal appearance.

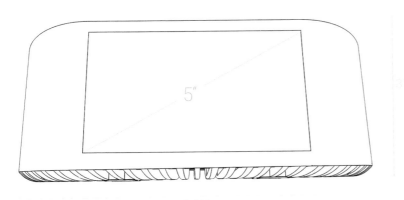

5"

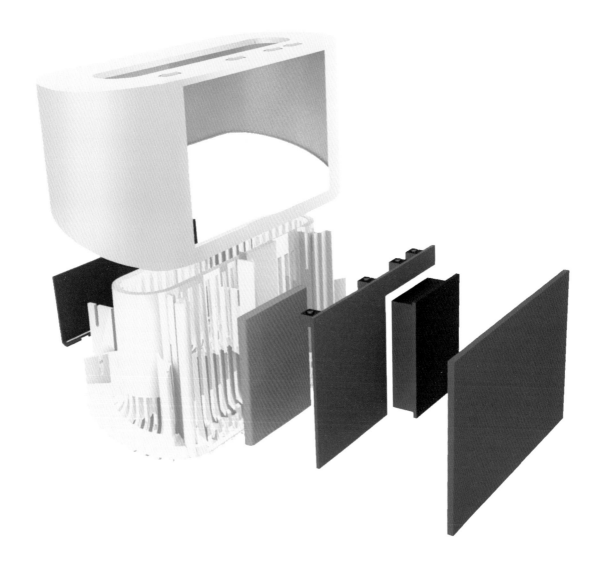

ThermoPeanut™

Co: Sen.se

ThermoPeanut™ is a smart wireless thermometer to measure temperature and improve energy efficiency. The two-inch sensor simply connects via Bluetooth 4.0 to smartphones and tablets through its dedicated iOS or Android app. Once registered, ThermoPeanut can be secured to any surface and the ideal temperature ranges for the area entered in the app. App notifications and sound alerts from the ThermoPeanut itself alert users when temperature readings are outside preset norms. Temperature status can also be checked anytime without a device by simply pressing ThermoPeanut, which will play a sound to indicate if the space is too hot or cold.

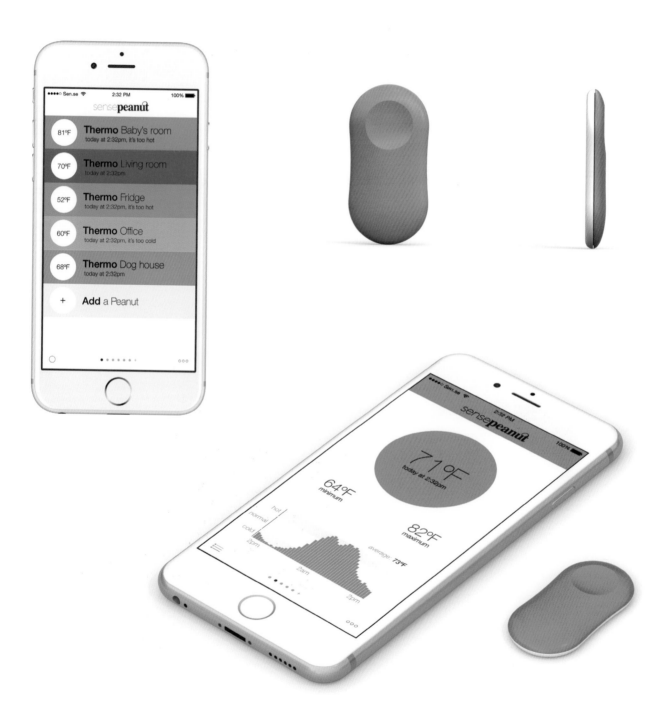

Mother

Co: Sen.se

Mother is a versatile sensor system. It includes an Internet-connected Mother hub and reprogrammable sensors. Small and slick, they can be affixed to almost anything. Using Smart Motion Technology™ they detect and analyze the specific movements of every activity. They can also measure temperature and detect the presence of people or objects at a defined location.

Each user can assign the sensors to the functions needed by picking an app in the available list: How many coffees do I drink per day? What's the temperature in my baby's room? What's the quality of my sleep? I want to know that my children are back home safe, etc. Sensors can be re-assigned freely and endlessly. It's like having dozens of devices in just one elegant solution.

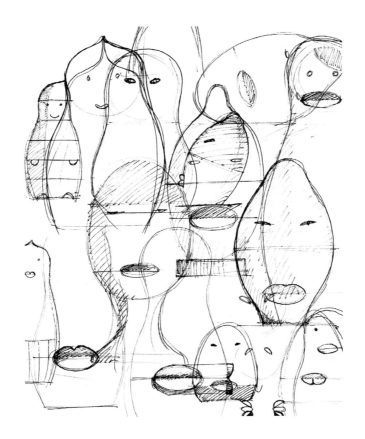

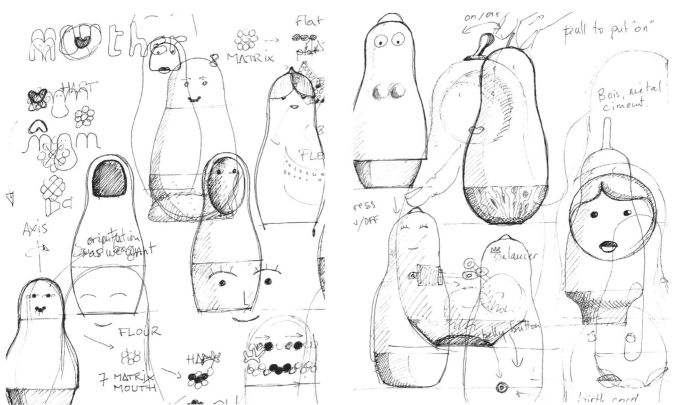

 Select the monitoring app you want to use.

 Place a Mother sensor on the appropriate object.

 The sensor will give you all the details about the monitored activity.

 You'll get notifications, reminders or alerts when needed.

GÖZ

De: Berk Ilhan

Göz offers a solution to bathroom related accidents, making the bathroom a safer place. Users can screw the bulb into any overhead light fixture, and drop the drain plug into any existing bath fixture. Both of these elements are designed to be inconspicuous and modest; thus users have no uncomfortable feeling when using the fall-detection alert system. The user then downloads the mobile app and selects which family members and friends should be called in case there is a fall in the bathroom. The smart bulb automatically detects falls using proximity sensors. Its built-in speaker and microphone—located at the midpoint of the bulb—turns the device into a 2-way speakerphone, providing a hands-free way for the injured person to communicate her or his needs effectively, and helping the people who are on the way over to be better prepared.

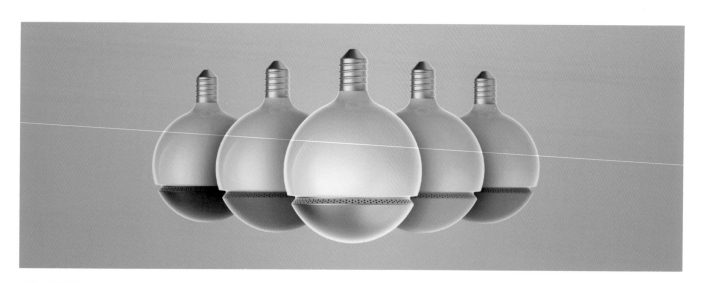

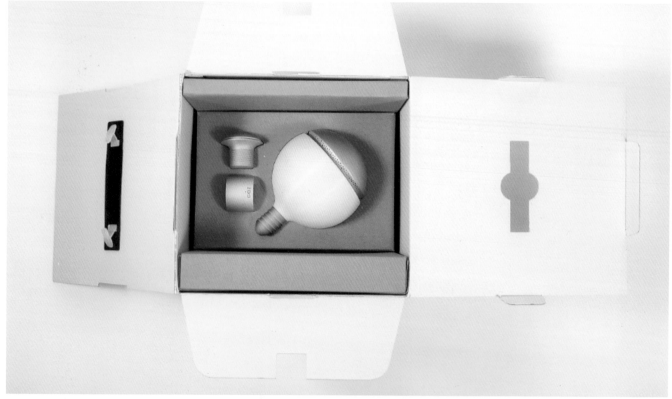

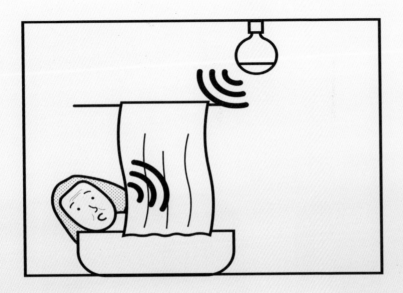

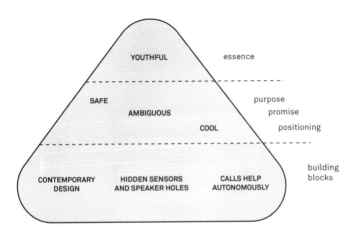

Blossom

Co: Blossom

Blossom is a solution for the waste issue of irrigation water. As a smart irrigation controller, the device works with a dedicated app, allowing users to control their sprinklers from anywhere. Blossom accesses hundreds of data points across your yard and determines a customized watering solution for you. Every zone will get a specific watering schedule based on your vegetation, sprinkler type and layout. Also, the device considers real-time weather data and gives users control right from their mobile devices, lowering their water bill and saving water.

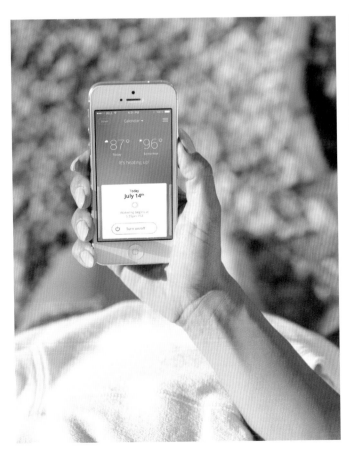

August Access System

Co: August

August Access is a platform for third party services to work directly with you for seamless home entry. Whether it's a shipping service, food delivery, laundry pick-up or a dog walker, your preferred service companies will be able to sync with your lock for seamless and controlled home deliveries. To fulfill its functions, the system consists of August Smart Lock, August Doorbell Cam, and August Smart Keypad.

The August Doorbell Cam, made of anodized aluminum, is a small and low-profile device that replaces your existing doorbell, and provides full visibility to any activity at your front door. Motion sensors trigger a camera built into the device, lighting up a doorbell icon on the device face. The entirety of the large August circular logo acts as the doorbell button. Once pressed, the camera feed goes straight to the homeowner's smartphone, providing real-time video and voice. Within the same screen, the homeowner can grant access, unlock their Smart Lock, and watch their guest enter or leave a package.

Enabling full access without the use of a cell phone is what prompted the design of the August Smart Keypad. It unlocks the August Smart Lock with the use of a designated code, a practical feature for owners and home services alike. The keypad is slim and discreet and the numbers don't illuminate until the sensor detects movement. Codes can be made permanent, in case the owner wants to access the house without a phone, or they can be temporary for one-time services or guests. The industrial design is meant to integrate discreetly into an entryway and is sized to fit perfectly next to the Doorbell Cam, with installation that literally takes moments.

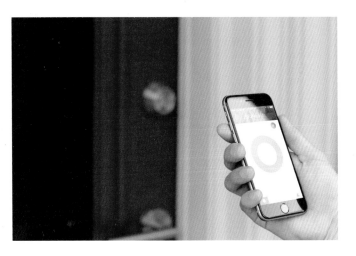

The August Smart Lock HomeKit includes the ability to use Siri™ to lock or unlock doors and check the status of doors using voice commands such as "Siri, lock my door," or "Siri, is my door locked?" on mobile devices such as iPhone. It is designed with a magnetic faceplate to easily access the battery compartment and HomeKit code, new micro-patterns to improve grip and rotation of the lock and a slim, chrome indicator at the top of the device so users can visually see if the door is locked or unlocked.

Triby

Co: invoxia

Triby is a portable, connected speaker designed for the kitchen and also functions as an entertainment and social hub. At the touch of a button, it streams radio stations and Spotify playlists with state-of-the-art sound quality. It also connects busy families who want to stay in touch throughout the day with hands-free VoIP and mobile calls and personal doodles on its connected message board. With In Vivo Acoustic® (invoxia's far-field voice capture technology) and the Amazon Alexa Voice Service, Triby allows people to access services from weather forecasts to adding products to their Amazon shopping list by simply using their voice.

Sammy Screamer

Co: BleepBleeps

Sammy Screamer is a motion alarm to keep an eye on stuff. Stick Sammy on the things you want to keep an eye on and she'll let you know if they move. Sammy bleeps when she's moved and sends a notification to your smartphone. For instance, stick Sammy to the fridge, and you can watch it and make sure that you're noticed when your children open it. When you don't need her, you can simply use the BleepBleeps app to send her to sleep.

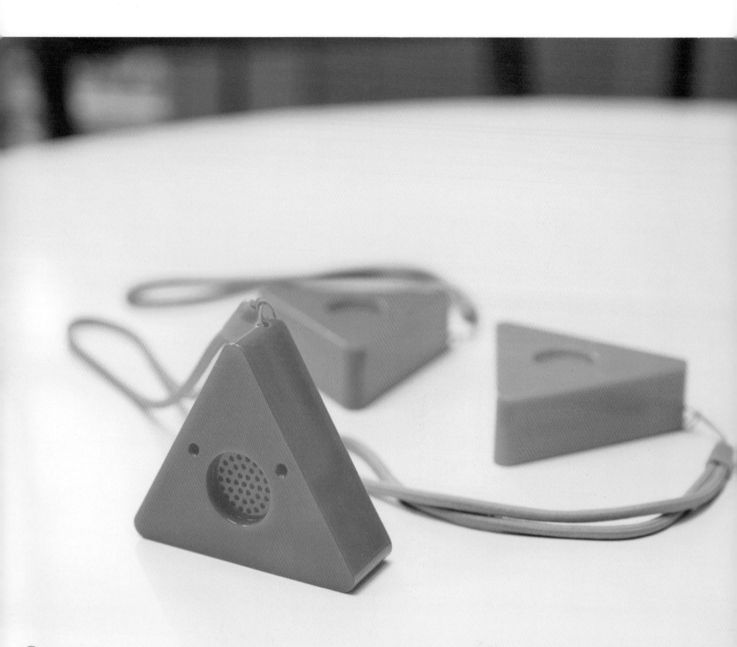

Cooc

De: Impel Studio

Cooc is a versatile app-enabled smart cooker you can monitor and control with your phone from anywhere with an Internet connection. It's a Sous Vide machine, a rice cooker, a roaster, a deep fryer, a steamer, and a yogurt maker. Cooc allows you to access recipes containing data that controls the unit for you. Temperature and cooking times are automatically set by the recipe program and adjust to your past preferences. More complicated cooking programs will generate a temperature-over-time graph, which can be monitored and manipulated to your liking. Recipe specific push notifications alert you when your dish is ready or when action needs to be taken.

Steaming Basket

Glass Lid

Double Walled Pot

Cooking Base

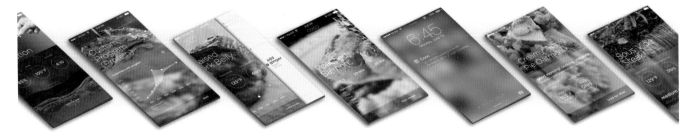

Pantelligent

Co: Pantelligent

Pantelligent is an intelligent cooking tool that controls cooking temperature and time. It is a smart pan with built-in sensor which syncs with an app. When you open the app and choose what you're making and how you like it, the app uses data from the pan to adjust the recipe in real time. And the smart pan then measures cooking temperature directly and warns you via on-screen and spoken notifications. You'll know when to flip, when to add ingredients, when to adjust heat and when you're done.

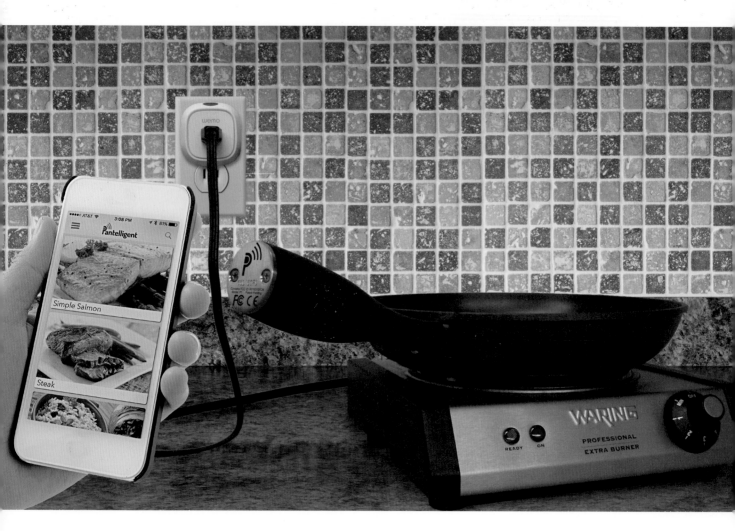

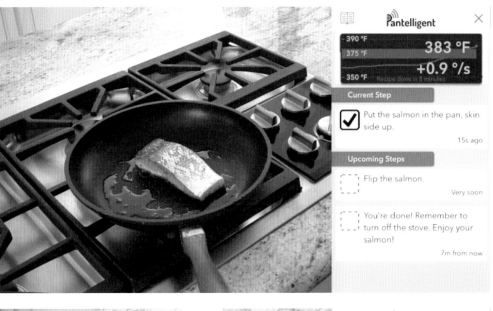

IKAWA Home Coffee Roaster

Co: IKAWA

IKAWA is a digital micro-roasting system to take control of your coffee at the push of a button and roast your own coffee at home. It provides specially developed roast recipes to bring the best flavours out of coffee beans. You can adjust the recipe to create your own perfect roast: change roast duration, temperature and even the air flow with your smartphone or tablet, and then share your recipes online through the app.

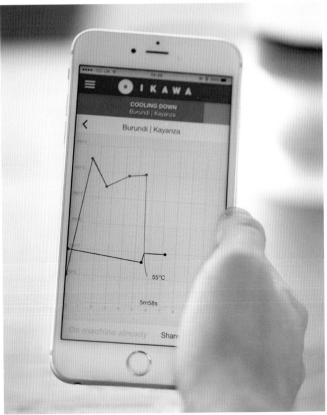

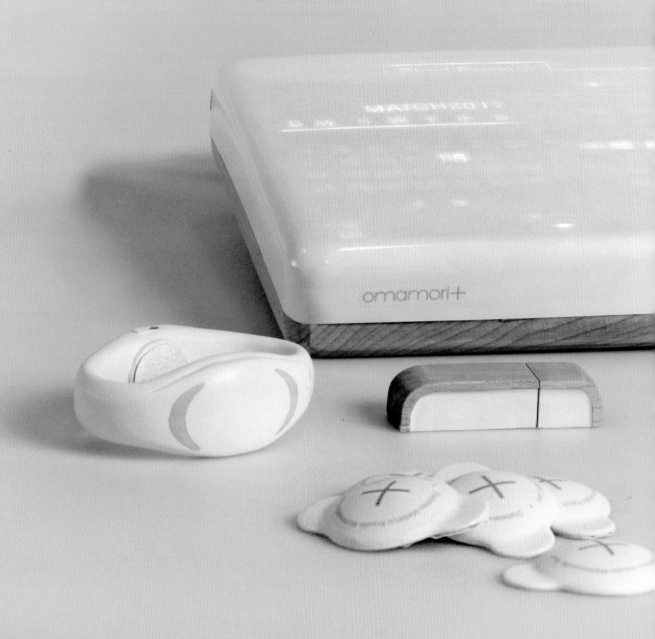

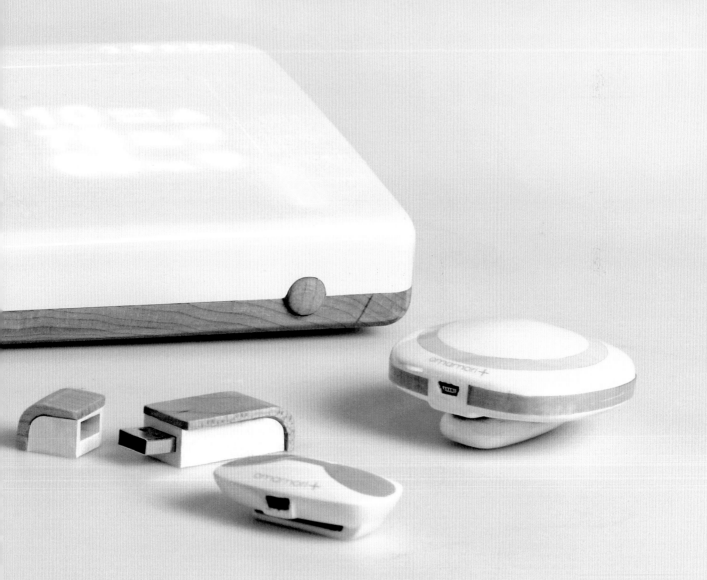

Health and Well-being

Omamori
Personal Health Monitoring Kit

De: Benson Lee

Omamori is a home based modular health monitoring kit designed for all ages to promote healthier living by bringing awareness to one's health condition. Omamori aims to ease individual medical reviews by reducing the frequency of hospital visits through simple data recording. It continuously monitors the user's health condition, warning them when readings fluctuate. The kit consists of a main device, a blood pressure monitor, a fitness tracker, a glucose monitor and insulin microneedle patches.

The blood pressure monitor uses radial pulse wave acquisition technology; the Raman spectrometer measures the diffusion rate of glucose into the interstitial fluid underneath our skin through a non-invasive method. Dissolvable microneedle patches are used to replace an insulin syringe. It is painless, while offering a much cheaper treatment process with the reduction of manpower and waste disposal requirements. Other common technologies used are rear projection of touch interfaces on opaque surfaces, haptic feedbacks, and also the accelerometer.

The devices are designed to be unobtrusive in one's daily activities. Individual devices are designed to cater to different monitoring needs, all part of a modular system. Data analysis and recording will be as simple as a few taps of your finger. The future of healthcare is within reach.

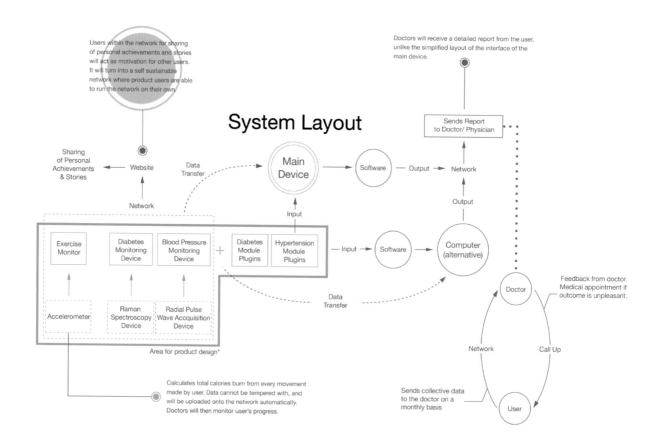

System Layout

Users within the network for sharing of personal achievements and stories will act as motivation for other users. It will turn into a self sustainable network where product users are able to run the network on their own.

Doctors will receive a detailed report from the user, unlike the simplified layout of the interface of the main device.

Sharing of Personal Achievements & Stories ← Website

Data Transfer

Network

Main Device

Software — Output — Network

Sends Report to Doctor/ Physician

Output

Input

Exercise Monitor

Diabetes Monitoring Device

Blood Pressure Monitoring Device

Diabetes Module Plugins

Hypertension Module Plugins

— Input → Software → Computer (alternative)

Accelerometer

Raman Spectroscopy Device

Radial Pulse Wave Accquisition Device

Data Transfer

Area for product design*

Calculates total calories burn from every movement made by user. Data cannot be tempered with, and will be uploaded onto the network automatically. Doctors will then monitor user's progress.

Doctor

Feedback from doctor. Medical appointment if outcome is unpleasant.

Network   Call Up

Sends collective data to the doctor on a monthly basis

User

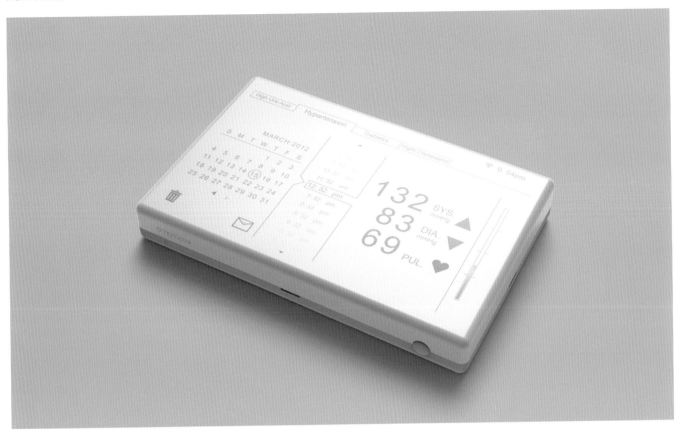

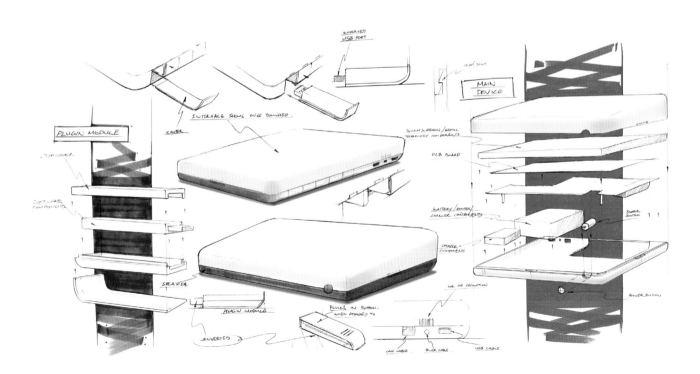

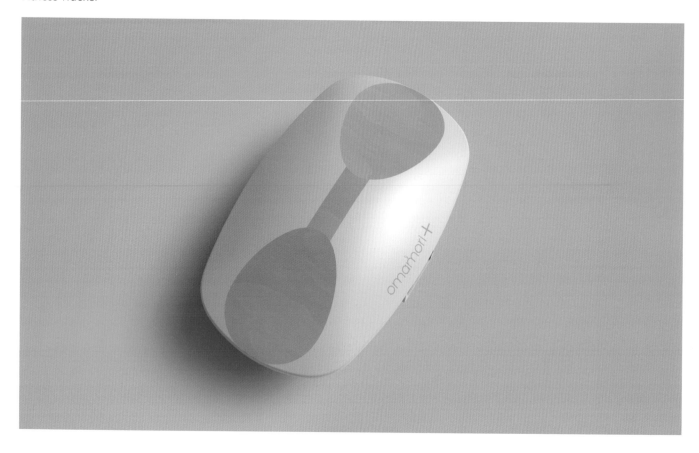

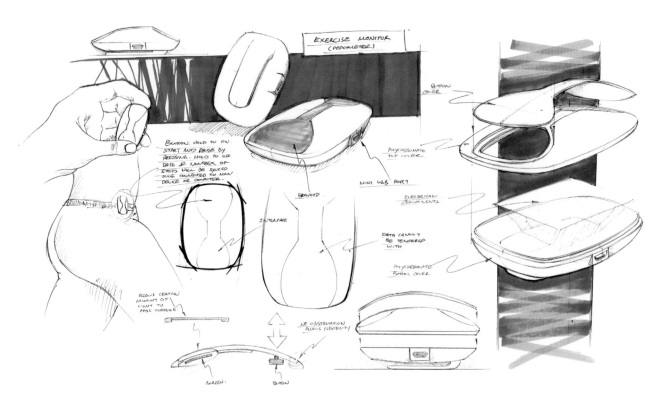

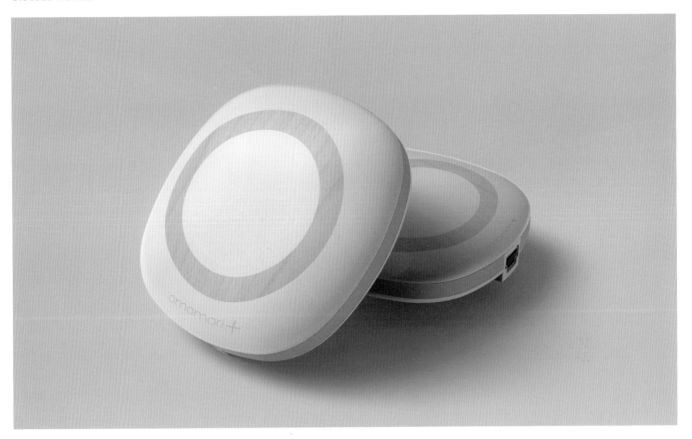

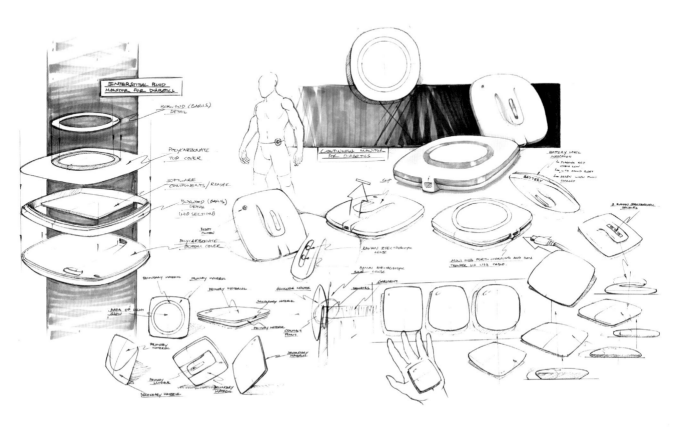

Blood Pressure Monitor

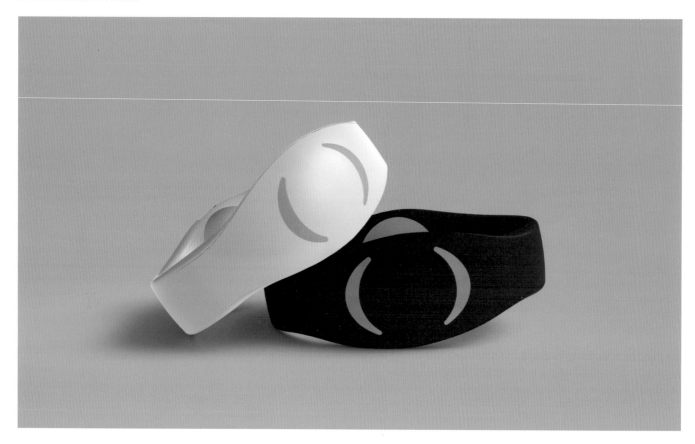

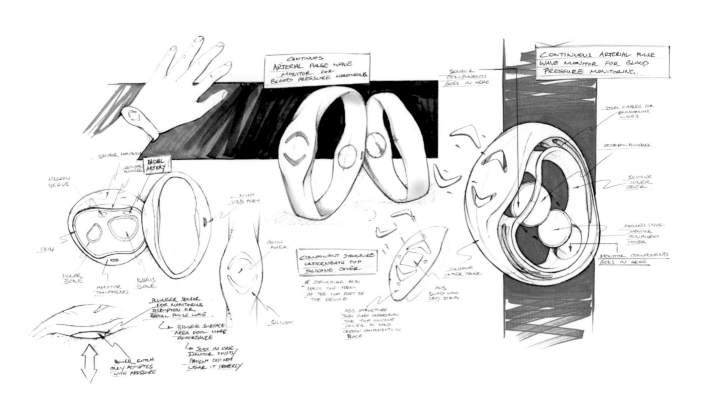

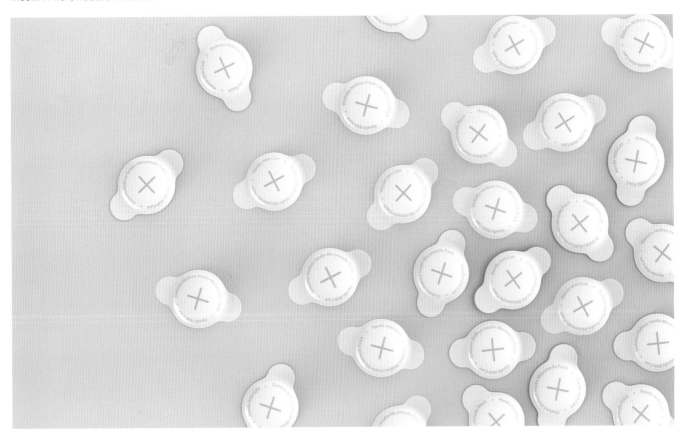

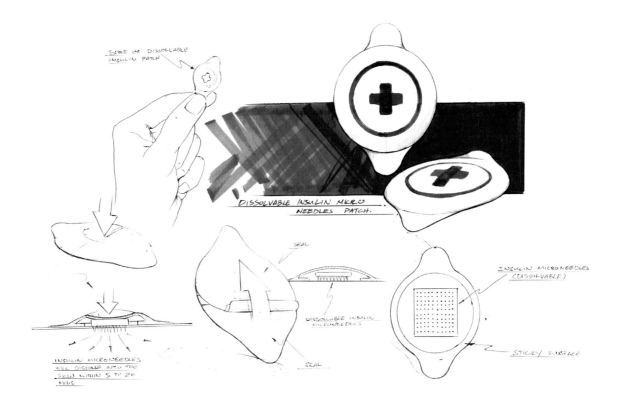

Nora

Co: Smart Nora Inc.

Nora is the first smart and non-invasive snoring solution, designed specifically to stop snoring before it wakes up your partner. It is a sleek pebble-shaped device that sits on the bedside table. Equipped with a smart sensor, once Nora detects the earliest sounds of snoring, it gently and slowly moves your pillow to restore natural breathing without disturbing the sleep of either partner. Paired with a mobile application, Nora keeps track of your sleep and snoring patterns. The whole system comes in a stylish portable case for travel.

What inspired you to develop Nora?

Nora was born as a solution to our personal problem with snoring. The inspiration for Nora came when Ali, a serial inventor and mechanical engineer, noticed how he and his wife dealt with each other's snoring: by slowly and gently moving the snoring person's pillow. He built the first version to mimic this movement and was impressed by its effectiveness.

After building the first prototype, Ali was joined by my brother Behzad and myself to transform the concept into a mass manufactured, user-friendly product. I had just returned from working as a Systems Designer with the San Francisco-based IDEO.org. With Behzad's knack for creative marketing and entrepreneurship, we had the right skills in place. We got to work, excited for the opportunity of bringing a solution to market that can help 40% of the general population improve their sleep.

Over the next year, the design was optimized in many iterations, and was repeatedly tested with different couples and in various bedrooms. The result is a user-driven solution that reduces snoring without waking up either partner.

We have received overwhelmingly positive results and great feedback from sleep scientists. With great initial validation, the team and advisors all saw the potential for enhancing sleep for millions of people. The project quickly gained momentum and in only 6 months, Nora received over $1 million in pre-orders from 75+ countries.

How did you balance product concept expression and market demand?

Market demand and product concept have been complementary forces in our process. With the benefit of a human-centered approach to product design from day one, we found ourselves iterating based on user feedback in each prototype round. While the minimalist and clean design concept of the product has not changed much from the original vision, we have made several tweaks to improve usability.

The sensor features a sleek look. Why this shape?

The sensor is the only visible part of Nora once it's set up in a bedroom. The organic shape is designed as an elegant addition to any bedroom setting.

Can you introduce the technology behind this "magical" device?

Snoring is the result of our airways collapsing once the upper throat muscles relax during sleep. When we breathe through this narrowed airway, we create vibrations that are heard as snoring. Nora's slight and gentle motion stimulates the upper throat muscles just enough to open the airway. As a result, users can breathe normally again. Rather than re-positioning the jaw, pulling the tongue, inserting ear buds or introducing more noise, Nora uses this ingenious method to stimulate the throat muscles and allow for normal breathing during sleep.

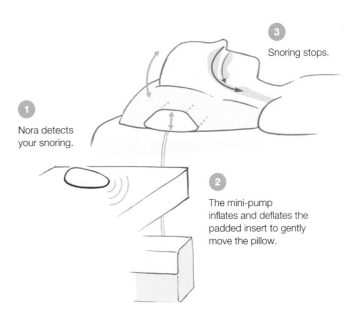

1 Nora detects your snoring.

2 The mini-pump inflates and deflates the padded insert to gently move the pillow.

3 Snoring stops.

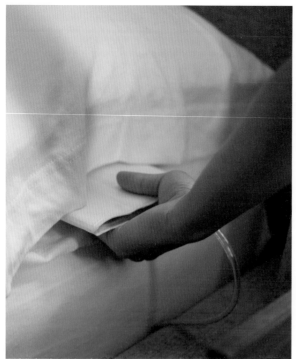

What benefits can users derive from Nora that they cannot get from competing products?

Nora is the first and only smart, contact-free snoring solution that's designed specifically to stop snoring before it wakes the sleeping partner.

Also, several of Nora's benefits give it a significant competitive advantage over the current market of anti-snoring devices. As an intuitive and non-invasive solution, Nora is a clear departure from the most prevalent solutions, including uvulopalatoplasty surgery, masks, and mandibular repositioning devices. Nora is discreet and requires no new bedtime routines or changes to an already familiar and comfortable bedroom.

Other products tend to focus on covering up the sound of snoring or create other discomforts as a side-effect. For instance, noise blockers mask the sound of snoring, but don't actually target the collapsing airway, which causes the snoring. Vibrations that alert the sleeper to the fact that they're snoring are also premised on the idea that there has to be some sleep-loss on the part of the snoring partner.

In contrast, with Nora the snorer's sleep is not disturbed by the gentle elevation of the head. Nora addresses the problem of snoring and simply fades into the background.

Nora is an IoT-based design. Why choose this concept?

At its core, Nora addresses the specific problem of snoring. But as we add features to the product, we will be pushing the limits of the sleep product category and explore correlation of snoring with factors like nutrition and physical activity. Since Nora is used every night, we will have the benefit of a massive database. In comparison to one or two night observation sessions in a sleep lab, this data will give much more to our research team to work with.

With the addition of the mobile application, we plan on analyzing sleeping and snoring data and alert users if they need to consult with their family doctor based on patterns that signal potential medical problems.

What do you think makes a good smart product?

We strive to design to improve quality of life. This aspiration is the same when designing services, communication, and products. Smart products are not really that different. A decade after birth of a massive smartphone market and affordable consumer products equipped with advanced sensors, the novelty of the quantified self gives way to clever and effective applications of the data we can gather about activities, environment, and bodies.

The bar for smart products has been raised and we believe products that go beyond information gathering and offer a tangible and effective improvement to the user's life are going to lead the way.

Are there any suggestions for startups?

Forget the romantic notion of suddenly quitting your day job and starting a business. Every business starts as a project. Take your ideas seriously, foster them, and be your own toughest critic. Ask yourself if your idea is really worth all the effort it will take to get off the ground. The only way to know is to start with small steps and let the success of your project convince you. You will know when it's time.

It's important to not lose sight of your original vision, but let early users and prototypes shape it along the way. Exposing the early design process to users significantly increases chances of success down the road.

Portal Telemedicine Headset

De: Jonathan Stewart

Telemedicine is a system in which a patient can communicate with a doctor online. The headset is used in combination with an online camera-enabled laptop or mobile device utilizing a secure software platform similar to Skype that provides the camera images and vital data to both doctor and patient. It also offers an appointment organizer, prescription issuer and medical history file.

The family kit includes a Wi-Fi/Bluetooth connected charge base with a storage stray for replaceable earpieces.

How the System Works

"The headset utilizes an in-ear pulse oximetry (PPG) sensor and tympanic thermometer providing medical grade data for heart rate, respiration rate, blood pressure and body temperature.

By utilizing a combination of Bluetooth and Wi-Fi modules, it also transmits images of the eye via a HD Eye camera and also independent localized imagery and audio from a detachable puck housed in one of the headset ear pieces. The data is securely shared to a health service server for GP access and algorithmic analysis. An opt-in scheme is also proposed to collect anonymous data for medical research."

Patient Interface

Doctor Interface

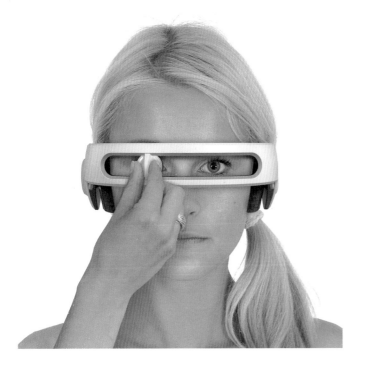

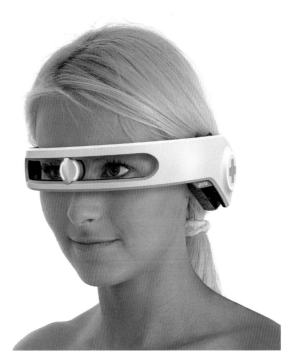

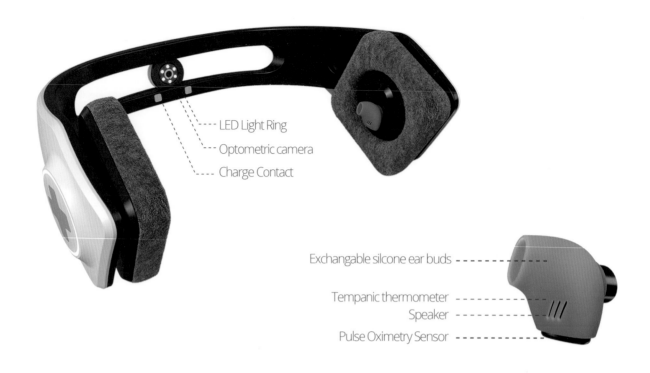

LED Light Ring

Optometric camera

Charge Contact

Exchangable silcone ear buds

Tempanic thermometer

Speaker

Pulse Oximetry Sensor

Wear Positions

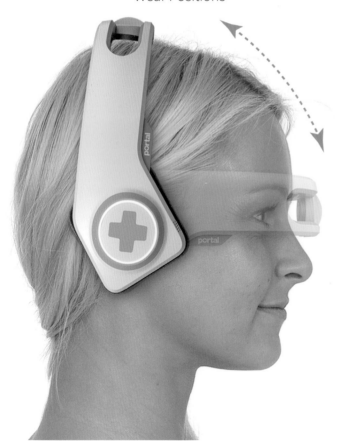

Size Adjustment

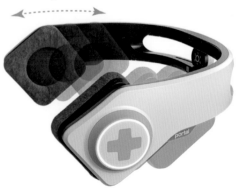

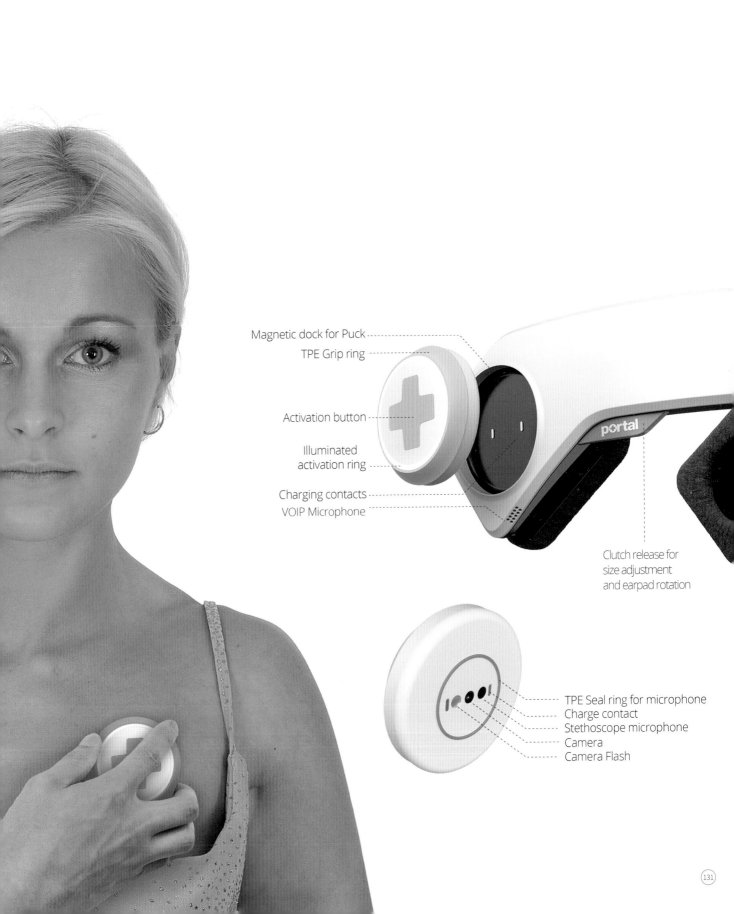

Magnetic dock for Puck
TPE Grip ring

Activation button

Illuminated
activation ring

Charging contacts
VOIP Microphone

portal

Clutch release for
size adjustment
and earpad rotation

TPE Seal ring for microphone
Charge contact
Stethoscope microphone
Camera
Camera Flash

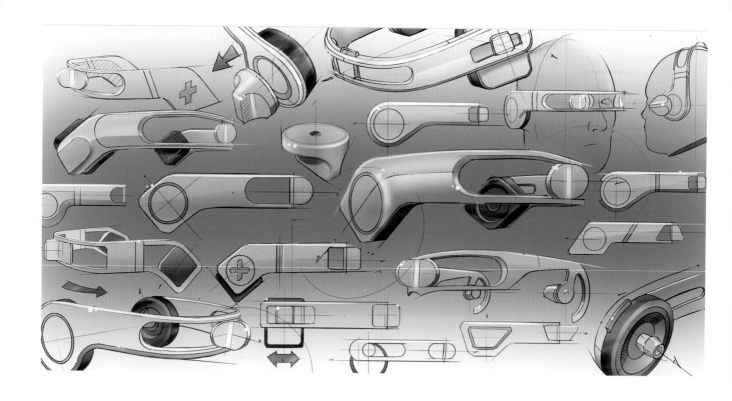

What inspired you to develop this concept? What was your main concern during the concept development?

The idea was conceived after a discussion with a relative expecting her first child; she praised the convenience of Skype consultations with her doctor during pregnancy—the time and cost saving stood out to her. She, however, required face to face consultation for physical data checks. This set me thinking about the sport wearable market where high quality, vital body data is collected affordably. It seemed logical to integrate the data collection technology with an online communication app similar to Skype and hence bring a technology currently servicing niche markets to a wider social application in telemedicine. During development, I focused on the primary data necessary in a standard checkup which beyond vital body measurements also included detailed images of physical ailments, the health of the eye and audio feedback from the chest. I also held heavy consideration towards the usability of the product as it would be engaged by a wide and varying demographic.

When talking about connected things, people are stressed over the privacy problem. Did you consider this when developing the Headset?

For telemedicine products to succeed, there must be trust; privacy and security is indeed of paramount concern in today's data-rich society. There were two aspects of privacy that I considered in the concept, the first being the direct environment and the second being online. One of the main reasons for selecting a headset format was that it enabled only the patient to directly hear the doctor's conversation in privacy. It was also of concern to me that the software must include advanced encryption and biometric login using the eye camera and/or face scan. The security of a system lies in its roots; therefore, I believe in the future there will be increased focus regarding the absolute security of encryption technology in system servers.

What are the next steps to make the Headset to be materialized?

Although the concept is currently technologically feasible, the greater task lies in the development of a secure software and database infrastructure. Going forward, medical institutions/healthcare bodies need to consider system wide implementation and a distribution model. To make the technology affordable to the widest audience that governments or private healthcare institutions could subsidize or rent the headsets.

Can you share your design philosophy?

The strength of a product rests in the designer's empathy with its user, both functionally and emotionally. I believe designers should think like actors, using their imagination to engage in cerebral role-play, shifting thinking to mentally visualize problems and solutions. This enables a platform of preparation before direct research that will corroborate or expose further insight in user needs and challenges. I believe good design should be rational and be approached as a logic problem with the goal of simplifying complexity and making the product experience feel intuitive. A product also interacts with us emotionally, whilst rational design naturally influences a form direction, tailored manipulation of surface, detail and color enforces an emotional connection with the user, the product should be connecting with us even before we interact with it.

Embrace

Product Development Pearl Studios

Embrace is a smartwatch designed to save lives. It features a revolutionary concoction of sensors and algorithms that make it possible for the device to detect an epileptic seizure ahead of time. This could allow people suffering from epilepsy a tremendous amount of freedom and relief, as they could prepare for the seizure and ensure they are in a safe environment.

Embrace is glorious in design, sleek and attractive, with nothing unnecessary on it. The cool, smart watch is targeted at general audience—from young to old, male or female. Wearing Embrace doesn't associate with its wearers with epilepsy, which makes the patients feel comfortable when using it.

Event Detection

Share Alert with Acquaintances

Event Notification

Monitoring Daily Activities

Data Analysis

Electrodermal Activity

Accelerometers

Temperature

Visualize Patterns

Clustering Comparisons

How Embrace Works

The Embrace monitors your activities and collects physiological data during day and night. The data then is analyzed in real time to give you feedback. The Empatica system analyzes historical data and interactions with your Embrace. In the future this will help you to discover patterns in your daily habits and behavior.

What was the biggest obstacle you faced during the development of Embrace?

Creating a wearable device that both saves lives AND is something the wearer can be proud of is very difficult. There are so many functional, manufacturing, ergonomic and other challenges that have to be packed into just the right package. This process is incredibly difficult and the results are very hard to achieve. In many instances we've had to re-invent how the manufacturing processes occur so that we can achieve the beautifully small package, while achieving great stability of data. This is further exacerbated by the requirement that Embrace must fit everyone. This means we must consider, at the same time, a 3-year-old girl and a 40-year-old man, and not only in fit or ergonomics, but also in style. The product, which appears simple, is a result of hours upon hours of creative thought and an incredible measure of essentialism: if it is not necessary, it isn't included. This process of elimination was critical in achieving what now seems a very clear product answer.

Did you consider the market demanding at the first beginning? How did you balance product concept expression and market demand?

Unlike most consumer products, Embrace is driven by the need for a better lifestyle of those suffering from Epilepsy. It isn't a technology we've considered matching with a consumer base, but an answer to a very real and serious societal issue. Because of this, the demand is tremendous. We've rarely seen other products where the customers are actually actively demanding we launch and ship sooner.

It's not convenient to take off wearable devices in the middle of the day and plug them in for charging. What are some power solutions in making wearable technology feel like a natural, consistent part of our lives?

We consider this very carefully. All of us developing wearable devices wish for better battery and charging technology, but the truth is, it's just not ideal yet. So, as a result, we have to carefully consider our feature sets and technology to align recharge cycles with functionality as well as normal behavior. In some cases, like Embrace, the critical need for the product trumps convenience. We need so much "juice" to run the algorithm, but it'll save your life. The tradeoff is worth it. We still try to optimize the charge cycle so that you can choose the best time of day, and we don't run out at any point in a single day. But in other cases, like in what we did with Misfit SHINE, we rethink charging completely. Instead of using rechargeable batteries in that case, we used coin cell batteries and worked extremely hard to edit the product so that we can extend the battery life to 4 - 6 months. This way, you never have to charge, and we remind you when to buy a new battery. Each product must carefully consider what is right for that use, then make appropriate tradeoffs. What's most important? What can we live without? What should be removed? And so on.

Privacy and security issues are still people's concerns when referring to smart devices. How did this affect your design and how did you reduce users' worries?

Digital privacy is always a concern. Security is something that is now part of every software developer's job description. At each level, from Firmware to Application to Cloud, we think about creating secure architecture. This should now be standard for all developers in this industry. However, there's always risk. This doesn't mean we should shy away from innovating; this just means we need to mature in our efforts to secure information and build tighter architectures, because the important products will really have positive impact on our lives. Therefore it's a matter of moving forward and getting better at what we do, not a matter of avoiding risk.

People today rush to produce "smart products" without considering whether it is really necessary to make a product "smart." What do you think about this situation?

Whenever a new industry is born, people flock to join the party. Of course, there are a lot of products made with exactly this mindset: "others are making sensor things or 'smart' things, let's also make something smart." We at Pearl don't believe in making smart things for the sake of making smart things. Every day new "tools" are made that enable us to re-think solutions to problems. Bluetooth, iOS, Android, accelerometers and other sensors are simply tools. Great products come from first having a need or an opportunity, then solving that opportunity better given the new tool. We ask ourselves, "Given we can now do X, what real and meaningful problem can we solve?" Unfortunately, some products are done by stuffing technology into a product, then trying to find a reason for it exist. Thus, we have a lot of products that are not useful.

How would you describe your design approach to someone unfamiliar with your work?

We feel design is a quest for a perfect answer to a problem. It is deceptively difficult and strenuous, which makes our lives even harder: no one understands how much work and thought is put into what people think are simplest products. Our approach is simple: we shower our work with love and passion. We focus on solving problems simply and elegantly, and we don't stop until we've achieved just that.

How will smart products affect our lives?

We think products in general have limitless potential. But they will do for us exactly what we intend them to do. So, if products are conceived as tools to make money—that's what they'll do. And if they are made to save lives—then that'll be the outcome. We certainly hope products we make will bring something positive to humanity: make more smiles, make days easier, bring more health or maybe even bring us closer together.

Vitastiq

De: Vitastiq

Dean Vranic: Creator of Vitastiq

Vitastiq is a compact, hand-held device that looks like a tablet stylus. It is made of titanium which gives it a sleek and modernistic feel and is compatible with most smartphones and tablets. Vitastiq communicates with the mobile app via a short wire and physical plugin. Together with the app, Vitastiq helps monitor users' vitamin and mineral status on a regular basis and provides them with basic information on 26 vitamins and minerals and their natural sources. With the app, users can look back at their previous readings to track their general nutrient trend and get an indication how their current habits might be affecting it.

What brought you to the idea of Vitastiq?

During some casual discussions with my friends—the other two co-founders—we came up with the notion that the devices that have been used for a long time to check the vitamin and mineral status (they are easy to spot in Croatian pharmacies and complementary medicine clinics around Europe) can be brought closer to the modern age. We were eager to put our experience and knowledge together and create the first personal gadget that helps track the nutrient trend.

Did you ever consider the market factor before beginning this project? How did you balance concept expression and market demand?

When we started developing the Vitastiq concept, we thought that it would be a great match for the healthy lifestyle movement and fitness tracker enthusiasts. To be perfectly honest, we did thorough market research but did not invest a lot of time regarding comprehensive analyses before we decided to initiate the project. After we considered all the current trends and statistics, we were quite sure that Vitastiq would find its audience.

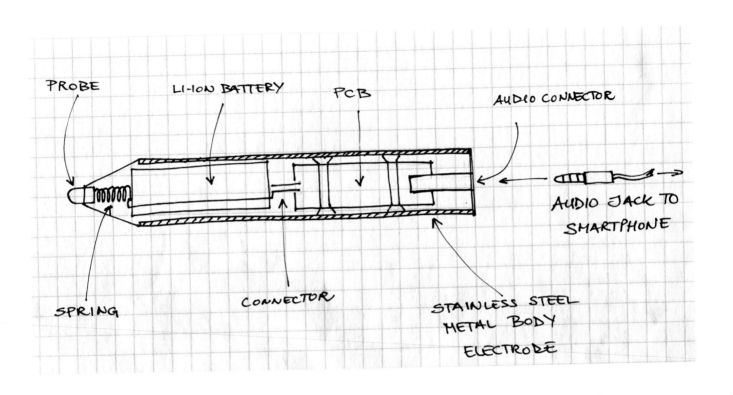

PROBE   LI-ION BATTERY   PCB   AUDIO CONNECTOR

AUDIO JACK TO SMARTPHONE

SPRING   CONNECTOR   STAINLESS STEEL METAL BODY ELECTRODE

What were your concerns when it came to the appearance design and material choice for Vitastiq?

When we first started, the idea was to make a device and an app for iOS only, so we adjusted the product to the "Apple Design." This was not an unexplored area for us, as we are ourselves inclined towards a clean and simple design, without any unnecessary details. Besides, we are a start-up company and we had to keep in mind that it would not be prudent to create a product with excessive production costs which we cannot cover. In addition, we wanted to keep the entire production process in Croatia, where not many similar devices are being produced. As a consequence, the technologies that we had at our disposal have, to a certain extent, dictated the appearance of the product itself. The result is the product that you see now. As a professional designer, I can say that I am quite happy and proud of it.

Vitastiq uses Electro-acupuncture. Can you talk a bit more about this technology?

Electro-acupuncture by Dr. Voll (EAV) is a methodology used by the professionals around the world for several decades. When Voll's team (and other experts in this field) was doing the research, it noticed that if there are any imbalances in the body this will be reflected in the electrical conductivity at the specific acupuncture point that is related to the imbalance. So what Vitastiq measures is the electrical resistance of a specific acupuncture point in relation to the general skin resistance.

Please talk about the aspect of Vitastiq that you are most proud of.

The method the Vitastiq is based on is relatively little known, so we had to devote a lot of time and attention to the user interface, but also to the explanations and instructions for our customers. Vitastiq's user-friendliness is a result of a joint designer-developer effort. Finally, our concept has gained international recognition in this field. Our team is truly proud to have received the Best User Experience Award from CESA (Central European Startup Awards) two years in a row.

What were the main challenges you faced when developing Vitastiq?

We wanted to make our device available to a wider smartphone-user audience. Therefore, we decided to connect Vitastiq with smartphones using the audio connectors, because that was the only type of connection that existed on all the phones (except on the new iPhone 7, which comes with 3.5 mm jack adapter). However, we were soon faced with a problem we did not anticipate, because on some models of the Android phones the port did not function the way we expected. As a result, we had to make adjustments to our Android application and customize it for certain smartphone models. It is very difficult to do so for each model on the Android market, and this was the main reason why we decided to additionally improve the product and come out with a Bluetooth version which, although more expensive, will be compatible with all the new smartphone releases.

What do you think are the main challenges and advantages of inventing smart, connected products in the context of Internet of Things?

Nothing exists in itself. We are all a result of our integration with the environment, and everything exists only in interaction with its environment. The better connected we are with our environment, the more profound our existence becomes. Therefore, the trend of the connectivity and interaction of products represents a logical development. The choice of Internet as a perfect communication channel is also quite logical. The products which do not follow this trend will not be noticed, and they will eventually disappear.

What trends do you see occurring in the field of industrial design with the implementation of IoT?

In general, with the advancement of technology you do not have to think as much about how to incorporate it into the product design, because the small dimensions and flexibility of the modern technology make it very easy for implementation. On the other hand, if the product works together with the app, this definitely affects the design of both the product and the app. It is only logical to align them, which entails adjusting the industrial design trends to those in the visual design of applications and vice versa. I would say that the virtual and the real are continuously intertwining and will increasingly continue to do so.

How do you think smart products and the related technology will affect our life?

People all over the world, including me, are already quite dependent on smart products. It is very easy to get used to better conditions and to technology that is working and thinking for us. But, does this make us better species with a better chance to survive on this planet? This is not so easy to answer. I would say that poor conditions and problems generally motivate us to strive for better, thus increasing our chances.

Technology will certainly continue to thrive, and I do not think that we have a choice there. Meanwhile, we as humans will become more comfortable and more at ease, and this is exactly the purpose of technology. If this eventually results in some enormous changes or even the end of humankind as we know it, we will all enjoy the view from the first row.

Dialog

De: Artefact

Dialog is a concept designed to help people with epilepsy gain a deeper understanding of their condition and make better decisions about their care. It gives them an easier way to manage triggers and thresholds, while it empowers them to use assistance from family caregivers, first responders, and clinicians as needed.

Dialog consists of a wearable module that collects a range of meaningful data about the patient and her/his environment, while a smartphone app provides the patient with insights into the factors that trigger events or lower thresholds. The platform can connect to the person's family and caregivers or even educate bystanders in cases of emergency. The easy, lightweight data input lets the patient log key information about her condition and subtle notifications help the patient respond better.

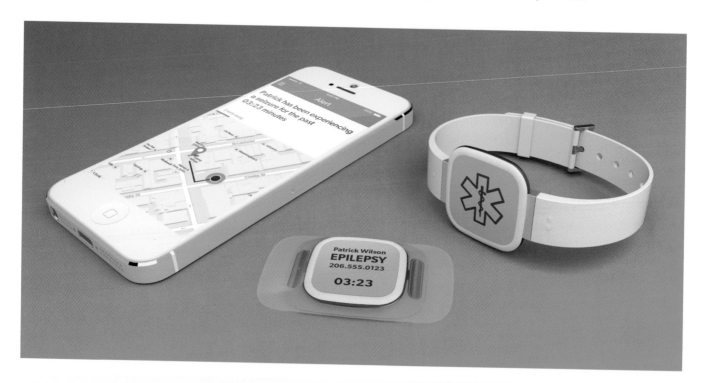

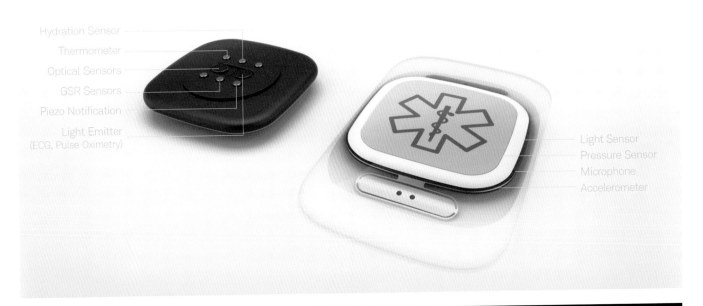

Hydration Sensor
Thermometer
Optical Sensors
GSR Sensors
Piezo Notification
Light Emitter
(ECG, Pulse Oximetry)

Light Sensor
Pressure Sensor
Microphone
Accelerometer

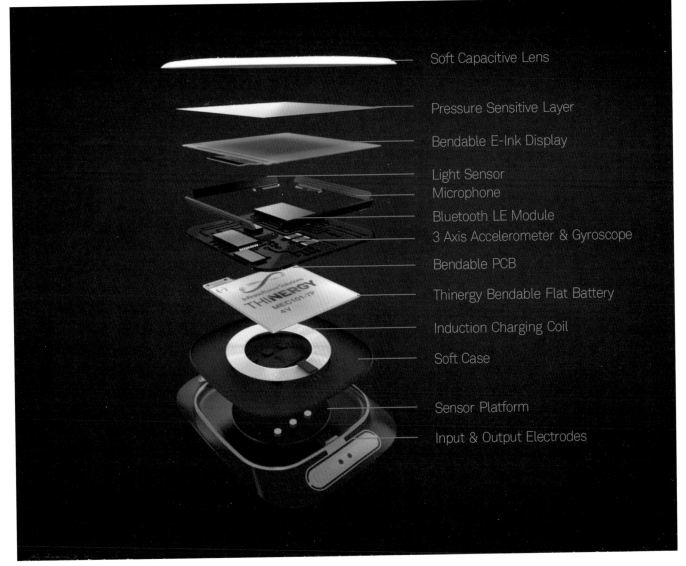

Soft Capacitive Lens

Pressure Sensitive Layer

Bendable E-Ink Display

Light Sensor
Microphone

Bluetooth LE Module

3 Axis Accelerometer & Gyroscope

Bendable PCB

Thinergy Bendable Flat Battery

Induction Charging Coil

Soft Case

Sensor Platform

Input & Output Electrodes

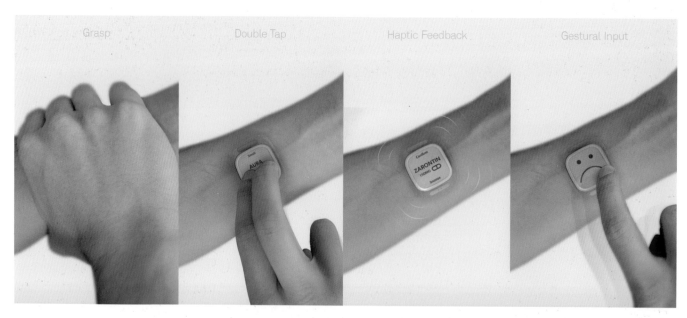

Grasp   Double Tap   Haptic Feedback   Gestural Input

The interaction language on the worn module is natural and uses different gesture types to signify different types of inputs and outputs. Grasp gestures (which may be all the patient can do while seizing) represent emergency calls for help. Double tap calls up aura input, haptic feedback subtly draws attention to medication reminders, and directional touch motions indicate moods.

System Overview

FAMILY CAREGIVERS

Send real-time
notifications and
updates

Connect via voice, video, or text

BYSTANDER

Display response
instructions and
log actions taken

CLINICIAN

Support collaboration
for understanding
condition and
changing therapy
through detailed
data review

PATIENT

Report details about triggers,
thresholds, and events

Send help beacon and provide instructions
Record contextual data (GPS, time)
Reorient patient to context after cognitive gap
Store data from multiple sources
Review past events and align triggers and onset

Record biometric
data in real-time

Time-stamp auras of different types
Track seizure onset and duration
Log mood changes
Manage medications with reminders

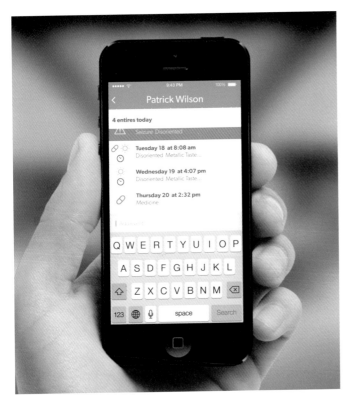

Co: WELT Corp., Ltd.

WELT is a smart fashion belt to manage users' health. Looking like a usual stylish leather belt, the smart Belt checks the body's current state with Waist Circumference (an indicator of health), steps, sitting time and the frequency of big meals of its wearers. The Belt then reprocesses these health data into a more actionable insight with associated health warnings. The Belt is a solution for people to embrace healthy habits while keeping in style.

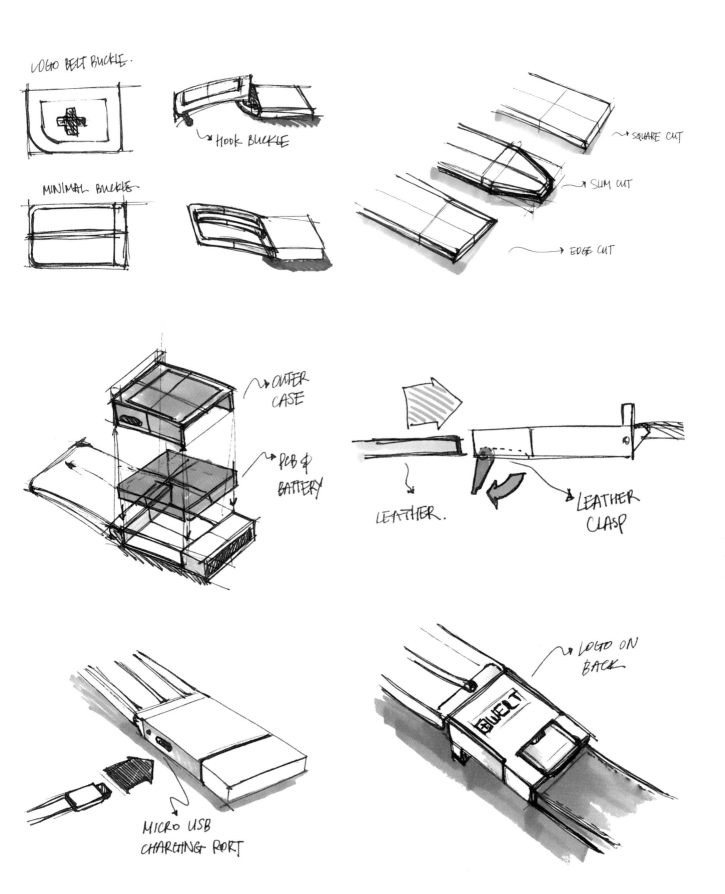

LOGO BELT BUCKLE.

MINIMAL BUCKLE

HOOK BUCKLE

→ SQUARE CUT

→ SLIM CUT

→ EDGE CUT

→ OUTER CASE

→ PCB & BATTERY

LEATHER.

LEATHER CLASP

MICRO USB CHARGING PORT

→ LOGO ON BACK

WELT

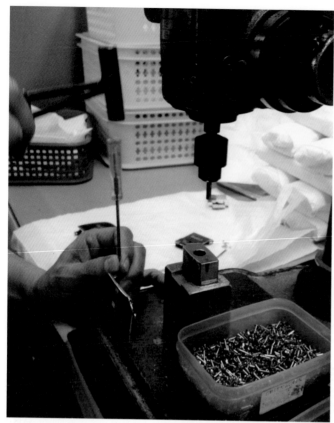

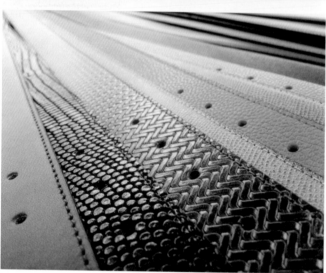

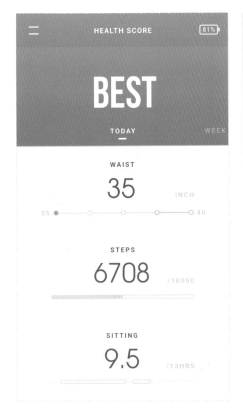

Nima

De: Nima

Nima is a gadget to help people lead their healthiest lives. The discreet and portable device contains two elements: the Nima body and the gluten capsules. The smart set allows consumers to test their meals for gluten anytime, anywhere.

Just fill the capsule with food and put into Nima; users will know the ingredients soon and avoid gluten food. Via the Nima app, users can also share their test results and see restaurant reports to find gluten-free places. Thus Nima alleviates users' stress from food restrictions, obtaining enjoyable mealtimes.

PAIR NIMA

Download the Nima app on Android or iOS to pair Nima. Check for firmware updates before running your first test.

HOW TO RUN A TEST

Recommended sample size. Do not overfill.

STEP 1:
Unwrap a new capsule and remove the silica packet from the bottom. Unscrew the cap at the top. Put a pea-sized amount of liquid or solid food into the one time use capsule.

STEP 2:
Keeping the capsule upright, firmly screw on the cap until you feel a pop. Keep twisting until the green ring disappears. Don't worry, you won't break it.

STEP 3:
Stand Nima upright. Slide the capsule into Nima until it clicks. The capsule will be flush with the top of Nima.

STEP 4:
Nima arrives charged. Hold the power button for 2 seconds to turn Nima on. When prompted, quickly push the button again to start the test. An icon on the screen will indicate the test has begun and if you listen closely, you will hear the Nima running.

= Less than 20 ppm of gluten

= Gluten detected

STEP 5:
Wait up to three minutes for the result to display. Throw the capsule in the trash after use. Do not reopen used capsules.

ZZZAM

De: HyeonCheol Lee

ZZZAM is a smart, connected alarm clock which is attachable to walls or bed heads thanks to nano-suction technology. The back plate of ZZZAM is flippable to the nano-suction pad which is attachable to any type of flat surface.

The smart clock tracks your sound, movement, and temperature when you sleep. Based on your sleeping data, ZZZAM wakes you up smarter, as well as gives you sleeping advice.

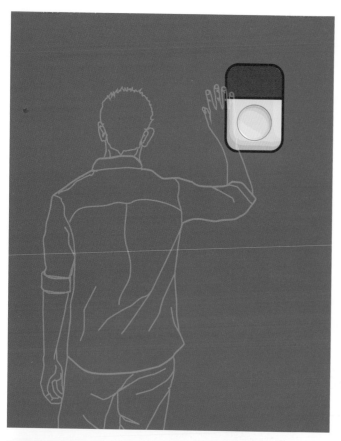
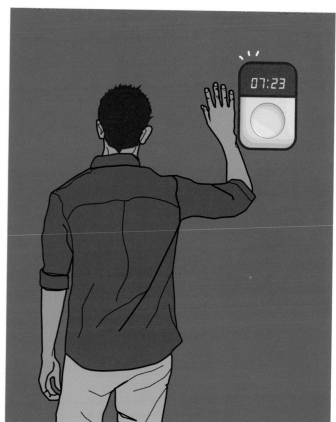

Responsive LED

LED responds to light, sound, and movement to save the battery

Hinged backplate

Backplate is pivoted and spinned to the red nano suction pad reverse parts

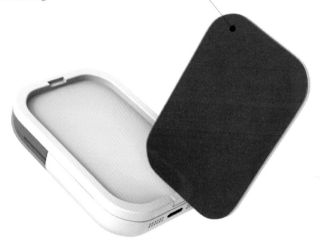

Micro suction pad

Milions of nano-sized suction cups make attachment stronger

Sleeping tracker

ZZZAM track your sound, movement, temperature while you sleep

360° Flipable plate

Spinned to the red nano suction pad reverse parts

Wheel button

The smart alarm and sleeping tracker only operates when the wheel button is pushed. To change the alarm setting, simply push the wheel button to release it. Spin the wheel until you find your target time; push the button back to finish setting the alarm and start the sleep tracker

Hibu

De: Francois Hurtaud

Hibu is a Bluetooth-connected wearable alert button. In case of emergency, its users trigger the device which then delivers the signal and location to those who care the most or to a predefined service, such as practitioners, fire station and forest guard. Hibu allows a button to be greatly reduced in size, and is designed to be worn in different ways. The battery for this waterproof device can last for up to two weeks and is easily rechargeable with its wireless charging station.

scenario

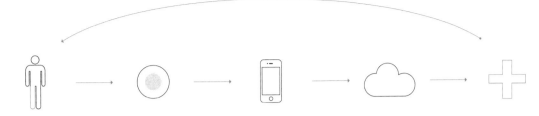

person

A person in an emergency triggers Hibu.

Hibu

Hibu relays the information to a phone via Bluetooth.

phone

The phone relays the information to the Monitorlinq server via Internet or GPRS.

Monitorlinq

The Monitorlinq server analyzes the information and sends the request to the dedicated service.

dedicated service

The service is alerted of the identity and the location of the person in need. The service performs accordingly.

inspiration

1. Gai Dan Zai Softness

2. Wearable Button

3. Single Trigger

4. Yoyo Playfulness

interaction

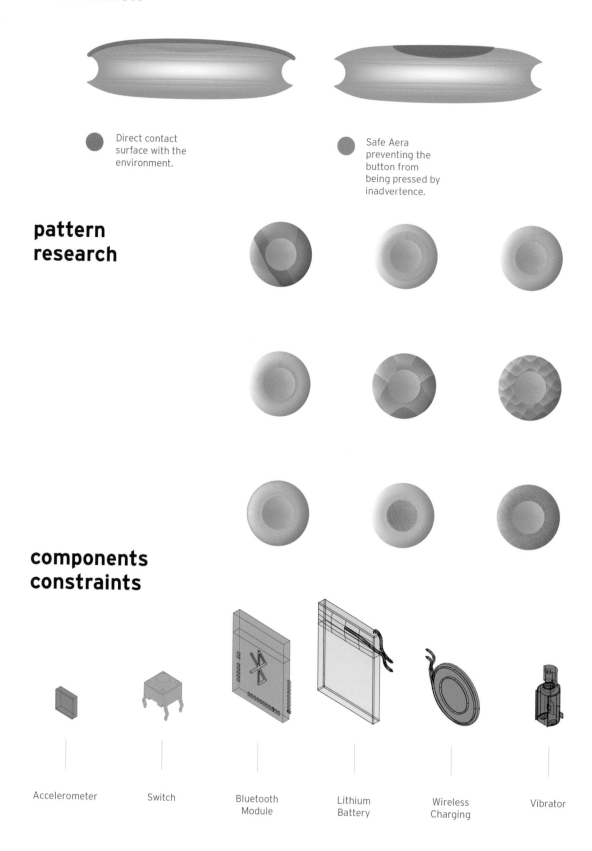

Direct contact surface with the environment.

Safe Aera preventing the button from being pressed by inadvertence.

pattern research

components constraints

Accelerometer

Switch

Bluetooth Module

Lithium Battery

Wireless Charging

Vibrator

Protection Ring

Key Holder

Necklace

Wirst Band

FitSleep

De: iFutureLab Inc.

Like a personal lullaby, FitSleep is a sleep tracker that uses alpha waves to help you fall asleep faster. It emits 0-13Hz waves during light sleep, speeding up the transformation to deep sleep, hence increasing sleep efficiency. The tracker also logs your heart rate, respiratory rate, body movements, and sleep patterns.

All the information the device learns about you will be stored and compiled in the cloud. After analysis of your sleep patterns and vital signs, FitSleep will construct a personalized sleeping report and provide tips to you for better sleeping quality. The device is so slim that you won't even feel a bump when it is under your pillow.

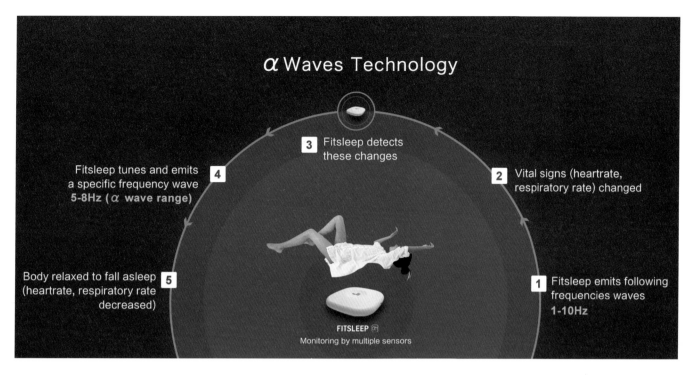

α Waves Technology

3 Fitsleep detects these changes

4 Fitsleep tunes and emits a specific frequency wave **5-8Hz (α wave range)**

2 Vital signs (heartrate, respiratory rate) changed

5 Body relaxed to fall asleep (heartrate, respiratory rate decreased)

1 Fitsleep emits following frequencies waves **1-10Hz**

FITSLEEP ②
Monitoring by multiple sensors

Co: Ava Science Inc.

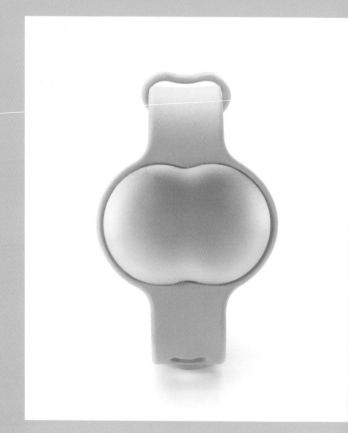

Ava is a fertility tracking bracelet that identifies an average of five fertile days per cycle, doubling your chances to conceive. There's no guesswork around timing intercourse or tracking ovulation.

Ava also monitors your general health and wellness while you're trying to conceive and throughout your pregnancy. You can use it to gain insight about your menstrual cycle as well.

LEAF is a smart jewelry piece which does everything a health tracker should do, such as measuring sleep, tracking activity, and monitoring reproductive health. Its leaf-shaped look inspired by nature makes it stand out from its competition. LEAF proves that health trackers can now be both functional and beautiful.

Neuroon

Co: Inteliclinic Inc.

The Neuroon is a revolutionary wearable device that combines advanced brain wave and pulse measurement technology with a comfortable sleeping mask commonly used in air travel. Using built-in biometric sensors, the Neuroon system analyzed your sleep architecture, calculates a sleep efficiency score, and offers optimization advice. In addition, the Neuroon mask uses Bright Light Therapy, a technology that can alleviate jet lag, improve sleep efficiency, and help the user to fall asleep faster. It also used an "artificial dawn" to wake up users with light of gradually increasing intensity, a function that reduces the unpleasant effects of morning sleep inertia.

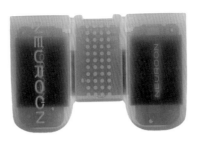

WiTouch

De: Katapult Design Pty Ltd

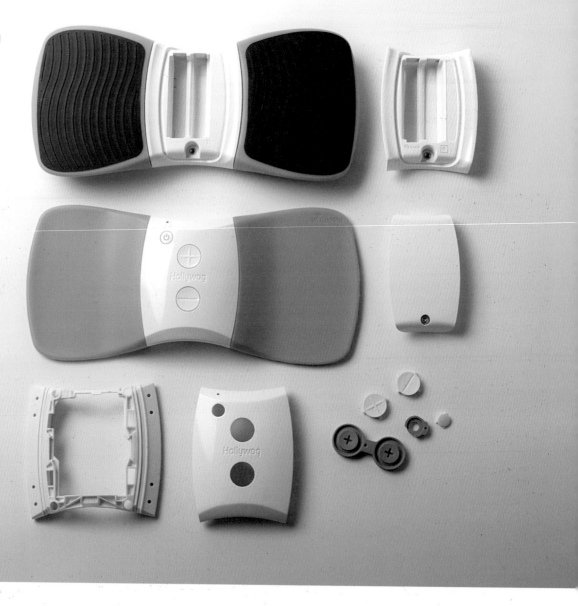

WiTouch is a highly portable wireless device that can be easily worn underneath clothes to relieve back pain. Its lightweight, flexible body adheres to the lumbar area of the lower back using hypoallergenic gel pads. The wearer activates a specific 30-minute electrical pulse treatment program using a small key fob remote.

The key to the design is the revolutionary use of technology and construction. Katapult used TENS technology in a wearable, portable format, creating a complex dual overmoulded body assembly that allows WiTouch to have highly flexible electrode wings that comfortably hug the body's contours whilst integrating a super tough structural skeleton to tie the product together and protect the electronics.

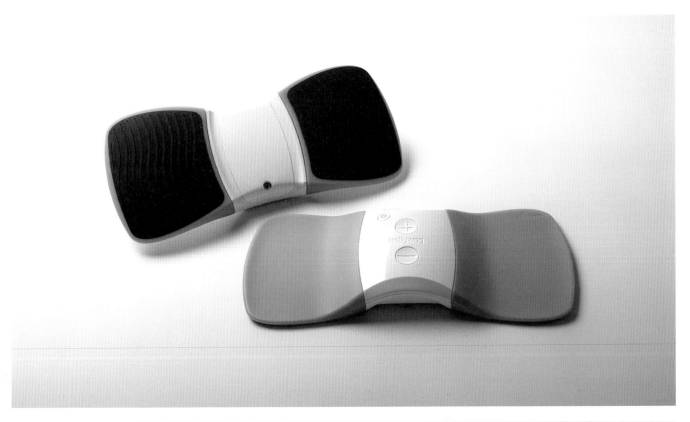

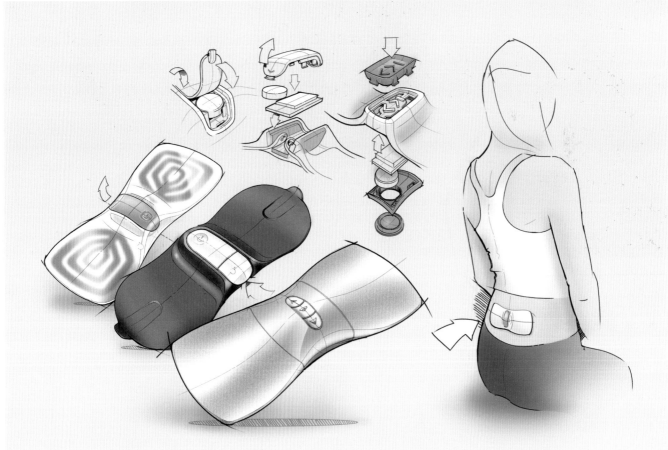

ALEX

Co: NAMU Inc.

ALEX is a wearable posture tracker and coach—a solution to Forward Head Posture (FHP) or Text Neck. ALEX doesn't treat your pain but instead addresses the causes underlying your pain by gently coaching you towards better posture. When you adopt poor posture for more than a few minutes, ALEX vibrates gently, encouraging you to improve. The accompanying coaching app will help you get the most from ALEX. It offers a number of unique features that help you track your posture over time and make improvements. Avatar Mode, for example, allows you to view and manage posture changes in real time. The app also provides graphs that track your progress of improvement.

Snuza

Co: Snuza International Pty Ltd

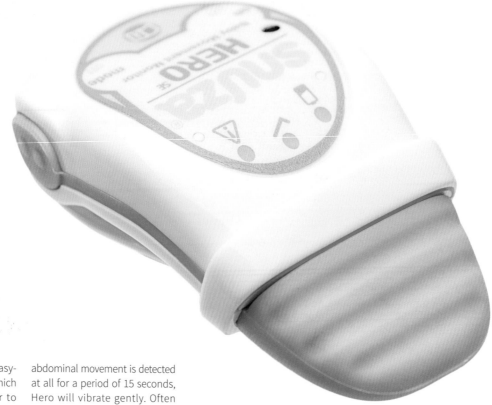

Snuza Hero® is a portable, easy-to-use movement monitor which clips onto a baby's diaper to monitor abdominal breathing movement. The Hero® detects even the slightest abdominal movement and will alert you if your baby's movements are very weak or fall to less than 8 movements per minute. If no abdominal movement is detected at all for a period of 15 seconds, Hero will vibrate gently. Often this vibration is enough to rouse the baby, and Hero will revert to monitoring mode. If no further movement is detected after 5 seconds, an alarm will sound to alert you.

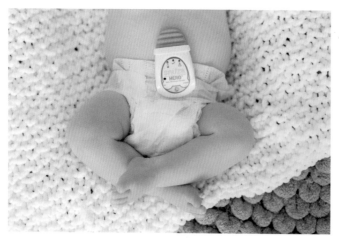

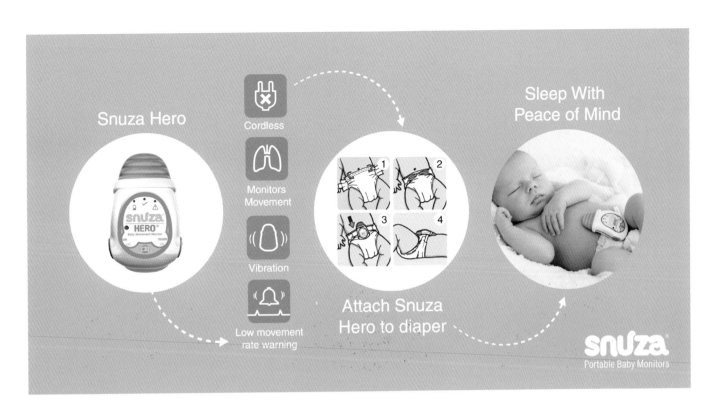

Snuza Hero

Cordless

Monitors Movement

Vibration

Low movement rate warning

Attach Snuza Hero to diaper

Sleep With Peace of Mind

snuza
Portable Baby Monitors

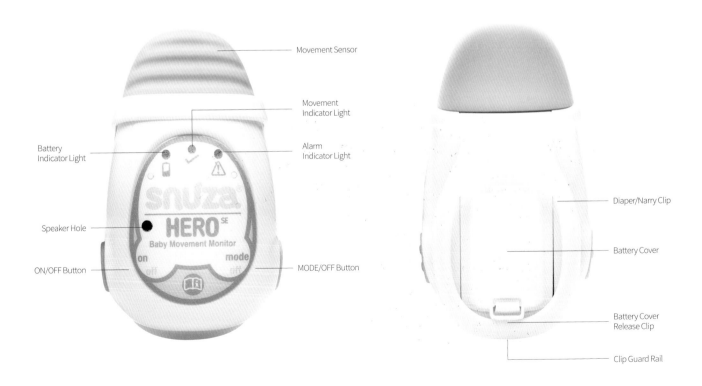

Movement Sensor

Movement Indicator Light

Alarm Indicator Light

Battery Indicator Light

snuza
HERO SE
Baby Movement Monitor

Speaker Hole

ON/OFF Button

on

mode

MODE/OFF Button

Diaper/Narry Clip

Battery Cover

Battery Cover Release Clip

Clip Guard Rail

Genesis Horizon

De: Arthur Kenzo

Genesis Horizon is a small, very simple emergency cell phone for seniors and children. It has unique wireless features that help caregivers save time, reduce stress, and better connect families. The Genesis phone only has two buttons. Hold down the main button to call the 24/7 Genesis emergency center. The Genesis phone has GPS tracking. You and the emergency center can find out where your loved one is. It will also alert you if your loved one wanders or arrives somewhere safely. Its medications reminder system alerts you when to take your medicines.

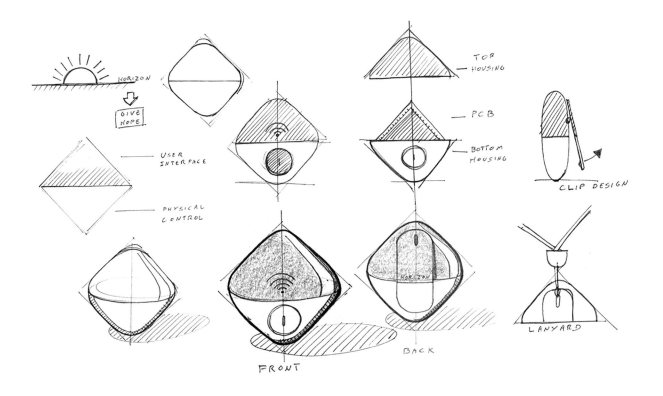

AirWaves Connected Mask

Co: frog

The AirWaves concept transforms traditional face masks with a particle sensor and Bluetooth connectivity. The mask monitors real-time air quality, and shares it via Bluetooth to an app on user's mobile device. The data can then be shared among friends and family. With such data, people know where and when it is better to go, or just stay at home.

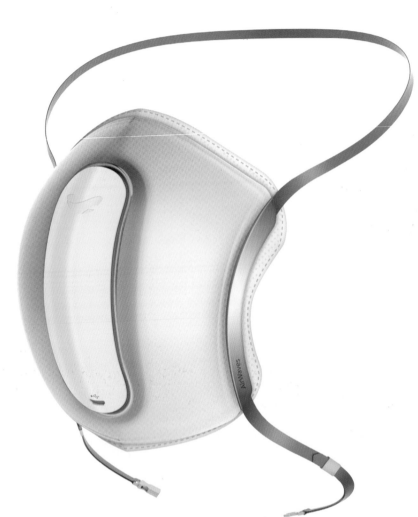

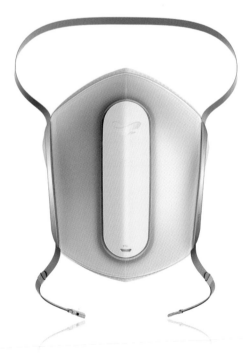

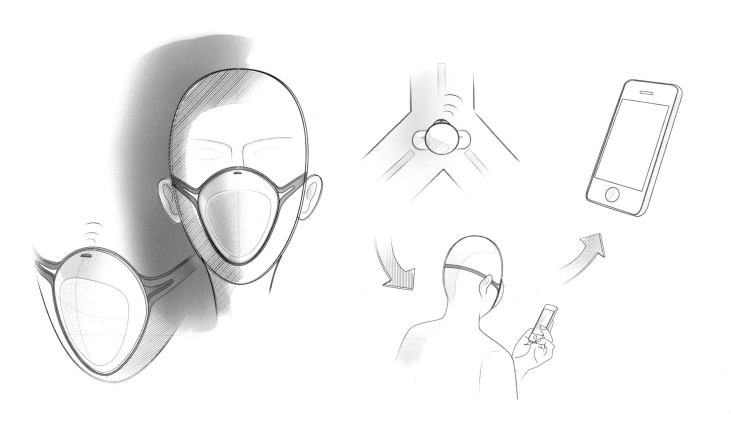

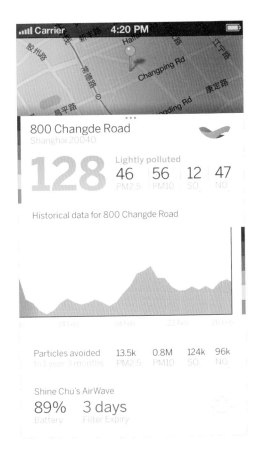

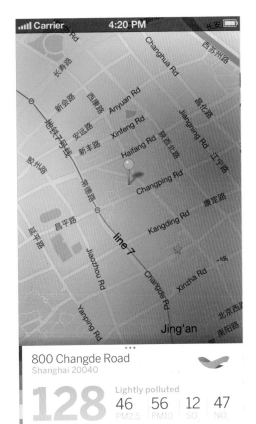

SCiO is a molecular sensor able to read the chemical make-up of materials. It is a non-intrusive, no-touch optical sensor analyzing many things, such as food, plants, medication, and oil and fuels. It tells users many things: how much fat is in any salad dressing, how much sugar is in a particular piece of fruit, and how pure a kind of oil is, etc. With every scan, SCiO learns more about the world around us, giving users instant information about the things they interact with and consume every day.

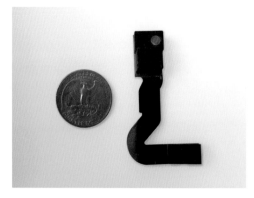

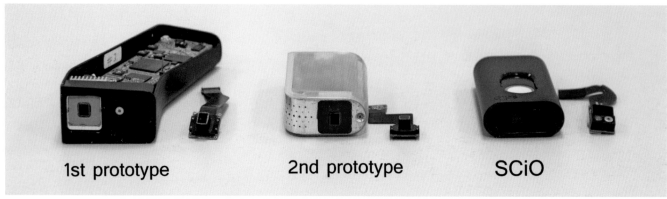

1st prototype   **2nd prototype**   **SCiO**

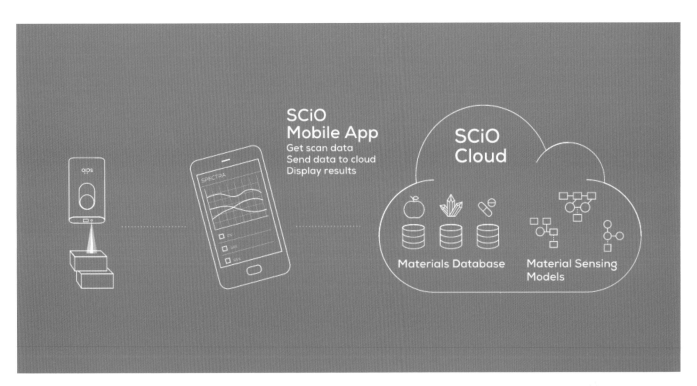

SCiO
Mobile App
Get scan data
Send data to cloud
Display results

SCiO
Cloud

Materials Database

Material Sensing
Models

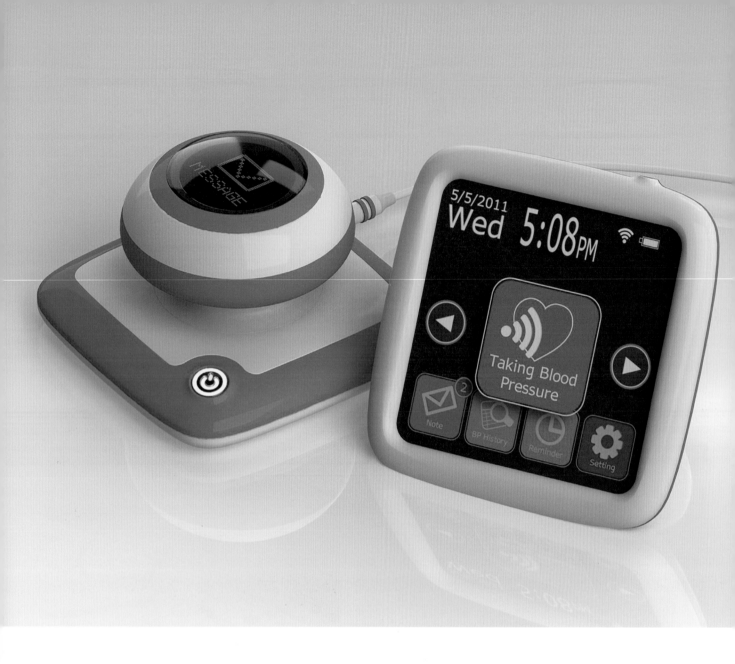

On screen: 5/5/2011 Wed 5:08PM Taking Blood Pressure Note BP History Reminder Setting

Bridge presents a conceptual design of a device that can be effectively integrated into healthcare medical services for the elderly. It is a smart blood pressure meter that can take blood pressure without the air compression cuff and share the information to practitioners by using the latest UWB technology. The device gathers medical diagnostic information and other important health data measurements, while being held in the user's hand. It will also remotely transmit patient information to medical practitioners, enabling real-time communication via alternate devices.

Bridge

De: Daryl Lin

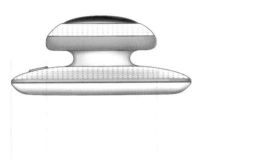

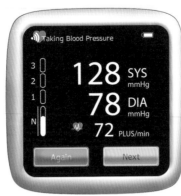

Taking Blood Pressure

128 SYS
mmHg

78 DIA
mmHg

72 PLUS/min

3
2
1
N

Again   Next

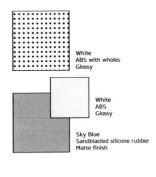

White
ABS with wholes
Glossy

White
ABS
Glossy

Sky Blue
Sandblasted silicone rubber
Matte finish

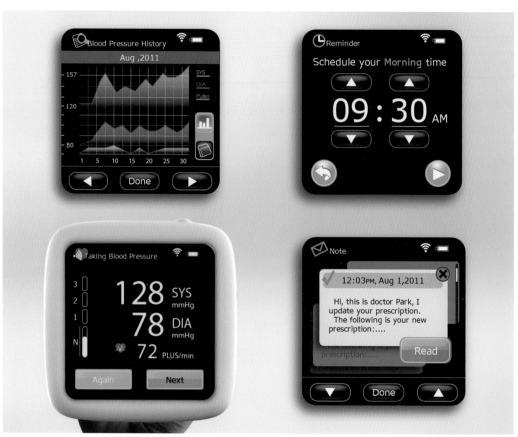

#	Part name
1	Ring
2	Lens
3	LED screen
4	LED screen base
5	LED screen holder
6	Handle enclosure #1
7	UWB module
8	Anti-slid cover
9	Handle enclosure #2
10	Screen enclosure #1
11	Screen enclosure #2
12	Speaker
13	Lithium ion battery
14	Bottom enclosure
15	Resistive touch screen
16	PCB
17	Power button base
18	Power button
19	Plug
20	Anti-slid ring
21	Data transfer cable #1
22	Power adaptor
23	Data transfercable #2
24	Vibration engine holder
25	Vibration engine
26	Vibration engine cover

Smart Consulting Service

De: Arthur Kenzo

Smart Consulting Service has been designed to reconcile patients and doctors in China where almost 3 billion visitors in Chinese hospitals and doctors are over-occupied and patients don't trust their doctors. The service is located at the hospital's entrance and allows people to register and pre-consult themselves before seeing a doctor. Except for providing advice and guidance, the human-sized virtual assistant will guide patients through the pre-consulting process, all the way from their personal information to their health recommendations. A touchable display, microphone and camera technology will detect people's disease and diagnose their vital signs. Once the pre-diagnosis step is completed, the service will guide the patient to make an appointment with the appropriate or favorite doctor. Smart consulting service will send patient's health information and first-hand diagnosis to their assigned doctor, therefore making the consulting process more efficient and enjoyable.

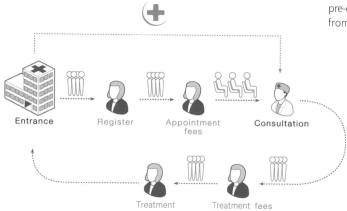

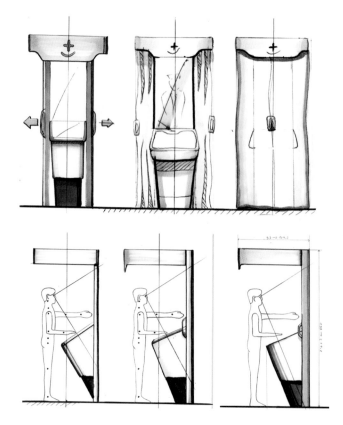

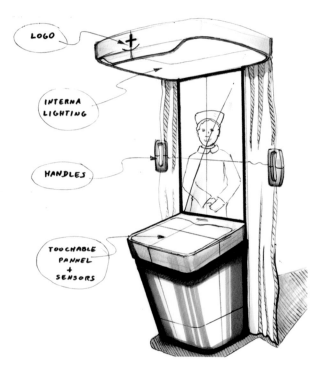

LOGO

INTERNAL LIGHTING

HANDLES

TOUCHABLE PANNEL + SENSORS

YONO Earbud

Co: YONO Health Inc.

YONO earbud is designed to provide the basal body temperature (BBT) of women by continuously monitoring overnight body temperature. When users wear it on at night, YONO earbud creates an enclosed and controlled environment in the ear canal, and YONO sensor captures the most accurate data without being affected by the room temperature, and it then measures and records the body temperature every five minutes. In the morning, when the YONO earbud is removed from the ear and placed on its charging station, it broadcasts the data to YONO app via Bluetooth. According to the temperature cycles and their peaks (BBT typically increases during ovulation), users identify when they are likely to be ovulating, which helps them to get pregnant or avoid pregnancy.

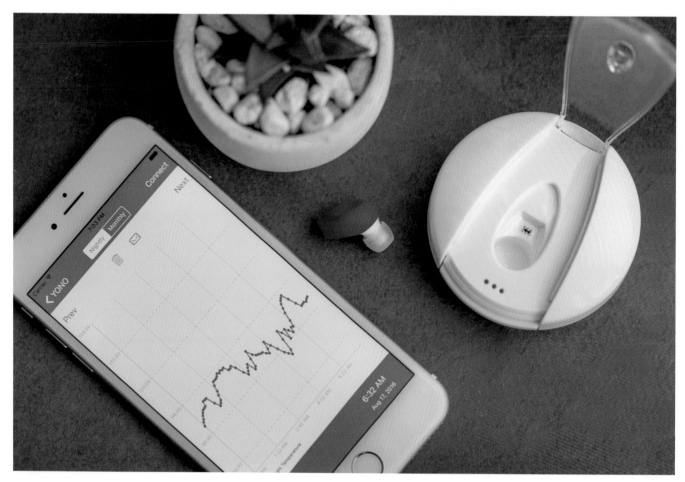

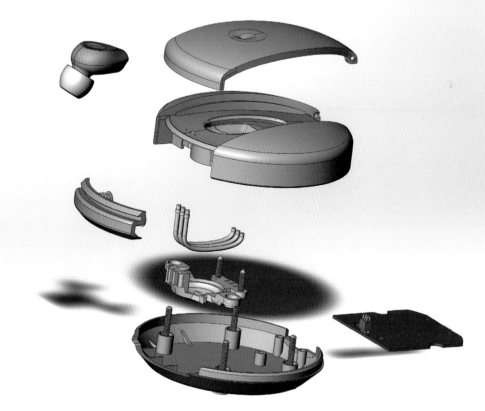

STONE

De: R&D Machina

Stone is a project aiming to improve public health quality. Unlike regular, hand-written carnets, the wireless NFC reader features an embedded chip that securely stores a patient's full medical record. This not only assists patients in a better way, but also empowers the efficiency with how information is accessed, held and managed across the entire public health care system.

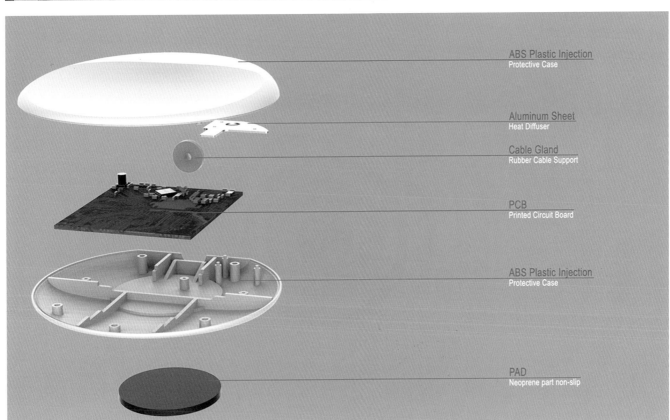

ABS Plastic Injection
Protective Case

Aluminum Sheet
Heat Diffuser

Cable Gland
Rubber Cable Support

PCB
Printed Circuit Board

ABS Plastic Injection
Protective Case

PAD
Neoprene part non-slip

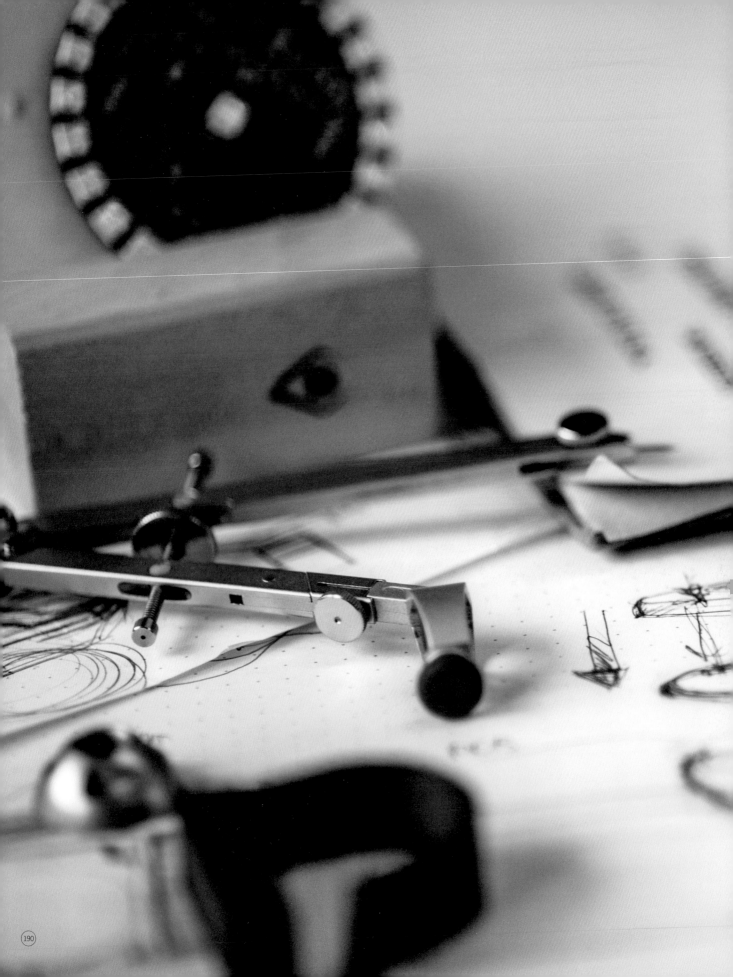

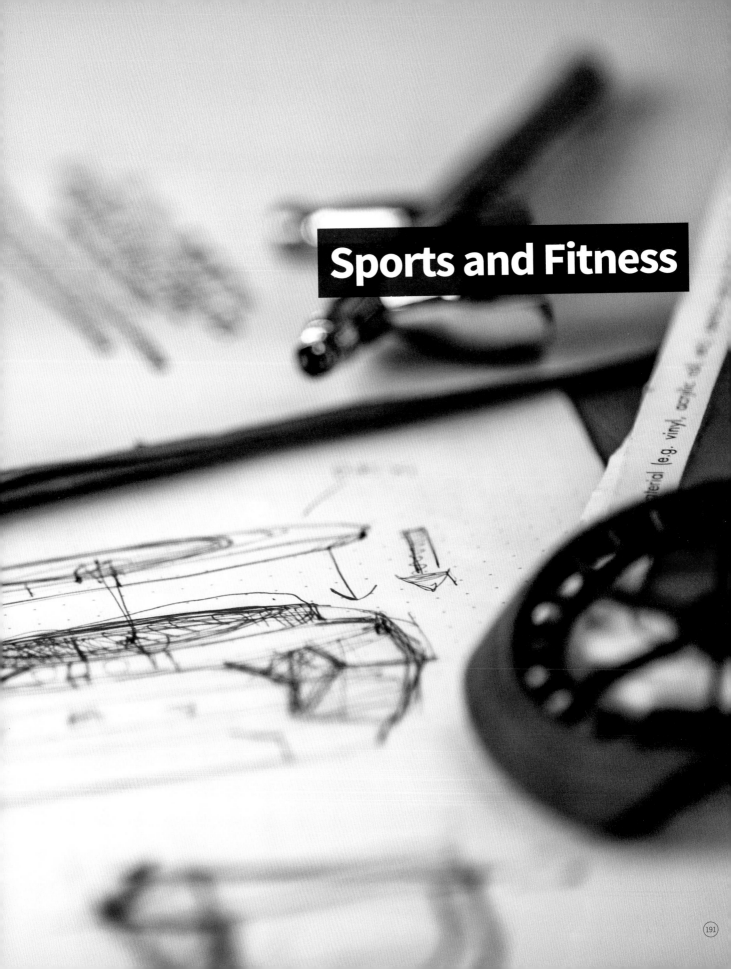

Sports and Fitness

SmartHalo

De: Maxime Couturier

SmartHalo is a smart biking device designed for urban cyclists. It installs permanently on your handlebar and pairs with your smartphone to provide turn-by-turn navigation through an intuitive and minimalist circle of light. It tracks all your bike metrics, lights your way at night and keeps your bike safe against thieves with its integrated alarm system.

What's the biggest obstacle you faced during the development of SmartHalo? How did you solve it?

One of the biggest challenges we faced was getting our locking mechanism right. Basically, we wanted the device to stay on the bike as much as possible while making it easy for the owner to take it off for charging. We could have worked with torque screws, but we felt it was a bit strange to unscrew the device so often. We worked with local partners to create an internal lock that works with a unique magnetic key and the final result is simply amazing.

Did you consider the market demanding at the beginning? How did you make a balance between concept expression and market demand?

We pitched it at just about every second since the initial idea to gather feedback. When we felt pretty confident, we launched a landing page to collect emails. We managed to finally confirm market fit with our Kickstarter campaign, which raised over 500,000 Canadian Dollars in 30 days.

SmartHalo is a device usually to the outdoors. How did you make it durable?

SmartHalo is made to resist any weather. We were strongly influenced by our city, Montreal, where the heat and cold can be extreme. The casing is water-resistant: you'll be able to bike under rain, snow or heat.

SMARTHALO INSPIRATION MONTLE

How would you describe your design approach to someone unfamiliar with your work?

We focus on simplicity and minimalism. Basically, we believe something is perfect when there is nothing left to remove. For example, SmartHalo's design is centered on simplicity. Biking in cities can be a challenge, so we've made sure our device was simple to use, yet smart. How? By reducing its interface to its simplest possible form: a circle. Such a slick and minimal look also makes it fit virtually any handlebar.

What do you see as the biggest advancement and risk in your technology sector over the next 5-10 years?

Sensors will become smaller, cheaper and more powerful. The next biggest step is to create technology that uses little power while delivering long-range communication. Think Bluetooth but with no distance limitations.

Many fitness devices have similar features in the market. How did you design SmartHalo to attract customers?

The problem with most fitness products right now is that they require some kind of input to "start" and "stop" tracking. Since our device stays on the bike all the time, it's possible to use the Bluetooth connection to detect exactly when the user is biking. That way, the collected data is always useful and relevant.

NAVIGATION

AUTOMATIC
TRACKING

SMART
NIGHT LIGHT

CALL
NOTIFICATIONS

ALARM
SYSTEM

Copenhagen Wheel

Design and Development MIT SENSEable and Superpedestrian, Inc.

Carlo Ratti
Director of the MIT SENSEable City Lab
Co-inventor of the Copenhagen Wheel

Assaf Biderman
CEO of Superpedestrian

The Copenhagen Wheel is an electric wheel that can be attached to most bicycles and turn them into an E-bike. The Wheel contains an onboard computer, battery, sensors and motor that respond to the rider's pedalling behaviour. The Wheel learns how bikers pedal and integrates seamlessly with their motion, greatly augmenting pedal power, which eases cycling.

An accompanying APP working with the Wheel allows cyclists to control the level of power assistance, track their journey and share data with other users. The sleek design and the impressive red-white color palette are a plus for the Wheel, presenting a result marrying aesthetics and function.

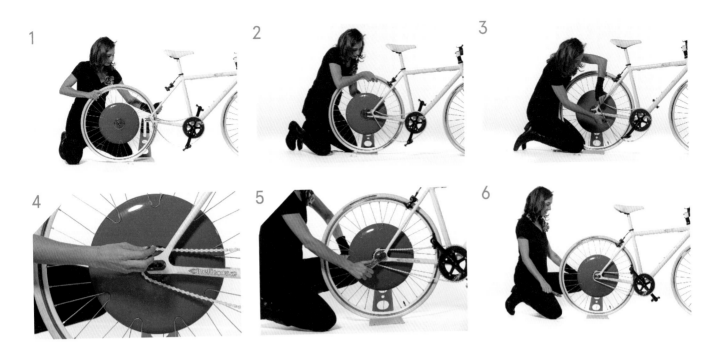

Can you talk about the idea behind Copenhagen Wheel? What does it mean to you?

Ratti: The project started as an experiment into human-powered mobility and air quality sensing in the city of Copenhagen. Our initial question was: can we transform any bicycle into a smart electric hybrid, by simply replacing the back wheel? The Copenhagen Wheel also allows you to collect data about your cycling activity (riding habits, calories you are burning) and about your surroundings (air quality, etc.). It is about bringing biking "online"—to promote feedback loops and inform urban change.

Biderman: We are interested in offering people a compelling alternative to the car: something that looks good, is fun to use, and is affordable. In addition to meeting people's daily mobility needs, we are interested in the emotions associated with the riding experience. To compete with the car, it needed to be captivating, and it is.
What we came up with is something that can transform any bike into a connected hybrid by simply changing the rear wheel. It allows the rider to cycle almost anywhere without worrying about getting to work sweaty or climbing that dreaded hill. The wheel models this interaction between a rider and their bike, and responds with added power in synchrony with the rider. It is a learning robot. We haven't designed a throttle for the bicycle, but something that organically integrates with how you move. The end result feels as if the wheel is a part of your body—something that becomes your riding companion, intelligent and noninvasive.

Upon the initiation of the Wheel concept, the interest in it is phenomenal. What do you think makes Copenhagen Wheel special and excite people? How do you balance the market demand (feedback) and the concept expression?

Ratti: I think the key concept here is the idea of human augmentation. Smartphones augment our interaction with others—the Copenhagen Wheel aims to do the same with cycling. In the end, this is impacting our very identity. Electronic prostheses get ever more indispensable to survive in the digital age, and we are becoming like cyborgs: humans augmented by technology.
Regarding the market demand, that was not our first preoccupation. Henry Ford once said, "If I had asked people what they wanted, they would have asked for faster horses…" In fact, since its invention, the wheel has evolved immensely, but stayed faithful to the initial idea.

Biderman: There's a massive search in the world for a new mode of transport to complement the car. Yet there hasn't been anything compelling on the market. The Copenhagen Wheel addresses this issue elegantly and efficiently. That's hard to beat.

The Wheel looks slick and beautiful; the color palette is simple yet impressive. How did you balance functionality and aesthetics?

Ratti: Beauty is functionality! In general we focus on usage—that results in objects that are both functional and beautiful.

Biderman: Simplicity is a guiding principle in the design of the Wheel. It's a circle with a minimal expression of form. For example, the spokes are embedded in the surface of the wheel to avoid the use of a flange, which would disrupt the continuous form. The installation is simple because it's a self-contained unit. The same is true for the controls, just pedal. The robot will do the rest automatically, seamlessly, and in the background. This made the Wheel a great challenge to engineer and manufacture, but it yielded the result we were after.

As an inventor, you have engaged in smart designs, such as the Wheel, Connected Kitchen and lift-bit. Can you share your design philosophy?

Ratti: We actually have just one focus , but one which is explored through different lenses: research, projects, products. We aim at being loyal to Ernesto Rogers' claim that architects should design "from the spoon to the city" —but while exploring the impact of digital technologies, which are part of what fuels our curiosity. In general, I am particularly fond of a dialogue in Truffaut's movie *Jules et Jim* between Jim and his professor Albert Sorel: "Mais alors, que dois-je devenir?"—"Un Curieux."—"Ce n'est pas un métier."—"Ce n'est pas encore un métier. Voyagez, écrivez, traduisez…, apprenez à vivre partout. Commencez tout de suite. L'avenir est aux curieux de profession."

Today people are passionate for designing smart, connected products. The Wheel also falls into the scope of the connected world. What do you think is the biggest barrier to make things connected in the context of IoT?

RATTI: In 1999, when the IoT concept was coined by Kevin Ashton, issues with deployment were primarily technological. Today we are connected everywhere—i.e., through our cellphones—but we just need to develop the right systems to transform this connectivity into something meaningful. Many people get excited about the fact that tomorrow your refrigerator and your TV could talk to each other, but what would be the meaning of that? Wouldn't that be the most boring conversation on earth? In fact, IoT has a meaning if it changes our lives, if conversations between objects help us better talk to each other.

Do you have a vision of a smart world? How would it be approached?

Ratti: I like the idea that technology might disappear—and then we will be able to focus again on the human side of things, as in the vision put forward by the late Xerox-Park computer scientist Mark Weiser. He presciently said, "Ubiquitous computing names the third wave in computing, just now beginning. First were mainframes, each shared by lots of people. Now we are in the personal computing era, person and machine staring uneasily at each other across the desktop. Next comes ubiquitous computing, or the age of calm technology, when technology recedes into the background of our lives."

How do you see smart technology will affect us?

Ratti: New technologies are radically transforming most aspects of our daily life. What I am particularly interested in are two aspects: sustainability and sociability. These dimensions are rooted in most IoT projects, and they are also central in the "sharing economy" paradigm.

TERA Fitness Mat

De: Lunar Europe

TERA is an interactive product concept that extends our exploration of how home training can be a compelling experience based around beautifully designed, behavior-inspiring tools for a healthy lifestyle. The physical incarnation of the concept is an intelligent fitness mat combining fitness and fashionable living in a harmonious blend. The carpet's intelligent surface with inserted sensors recognizes movement patterns and transforms seamlessly into an exercise mat, activating a dedicated TERA app. TERA shifts from a design object into a piece of individual high-tech exercise equipment with a multitude of functions.

Materials and Shape

TERA uses eco-friendly shear wool, a kind of wear- and slip-resistant fabric by premium manufacturer Kvadrat. The materials make for an elegant carpet that blends into any contemporary interior. For its shape, the mat is deliberately designed to be circular to accommodate the natural radius of human motion during exercise, making transitions between poses and keeping up the flow of the practice easier.

How Hardware and Software Interact

The paired TERA app is designed to be intuitive and in sync with the smart carpet. Accessing the app, exercisers are guided to training units of different disciplines, like Yoga, Pilates or Thai Bo, all with varying degrees of difficulty. When users exercise, the sensors inside will register any pressure exerted on the carpet, enabling accurate detection of the user's body and weight shifts. An innovative LED lighting system shows how to perform the exercises correctly on the mat, while sensors record the training units, which are subsequently analyzed with the TERA app. The training data can also be shared with a personal trainer in social media networks.

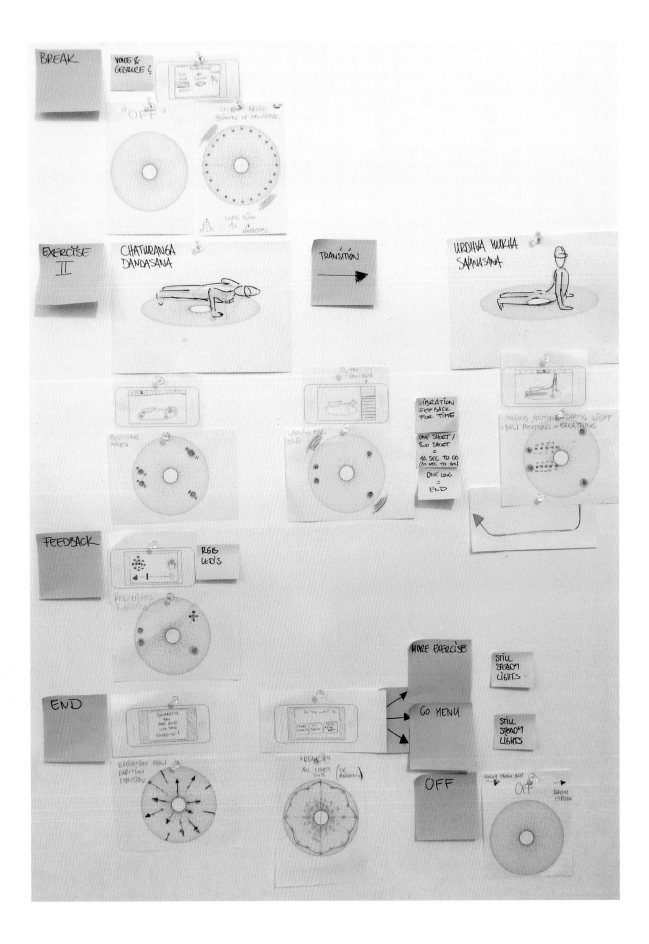

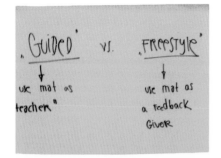

"GUIDED" vs. "FREESTYLE"

use mat as "teacher"

use mat as a feedback giver

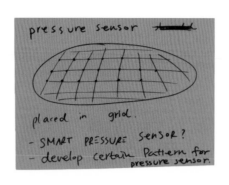

pressure sensor

placed in grid.

- SMART PRESSURE SENSOR?
- develop certain pattern for pressure sensor.

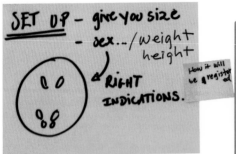

SET UP - give you size
- sex.../weight height

RIGHT INDICATIONS.

How it will be registered

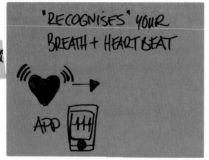

"RECOGNISES" YOUR BREATH + HEARTBEAT

APP

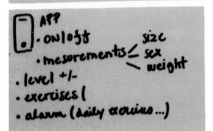

APP
• on/off
• mesurements ⟨ size sex weight
• level +/-
• exercises (
• alarm (daily exercises...)

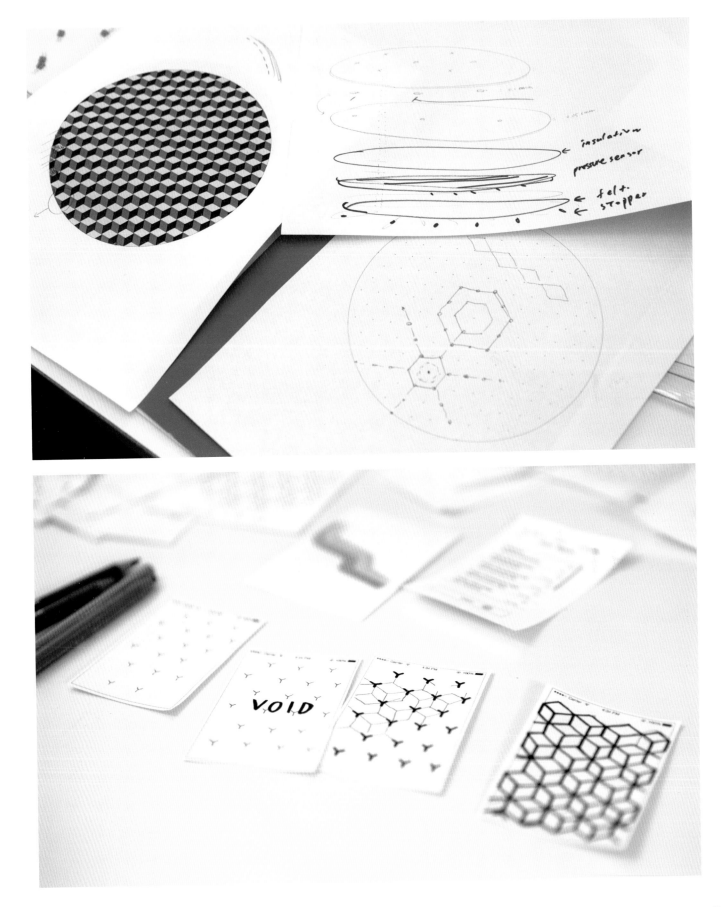

insulation
pressure sensor
felt.
stopper

VOID

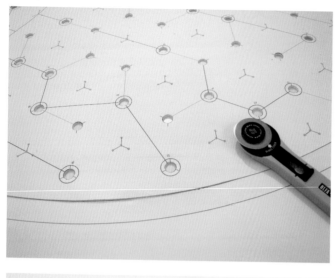

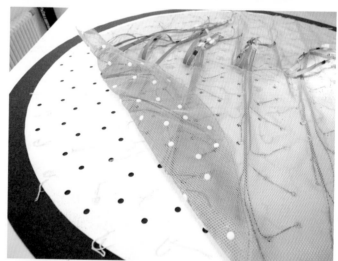
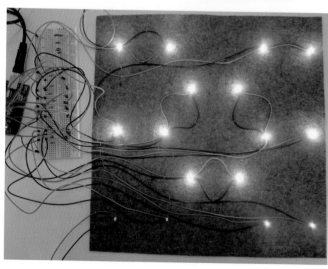

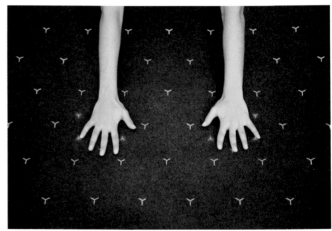

Sensoria Smart Socks

Co: Sensoria Fitness Inc.

The Sensoria® Fitness Socks are smart socks infused with textile pressure sensors that can help you improve your running form. The Sensoria Fitness app real-time audio feedback will track foot landing, cadence and foot contact time on the ground. Sensoria Smart Socks not only tell users how far and how fast they run, but how well they run.

Inspiration

The existence of the socks should be tracked back to the visit of Mario Esposito (the CTO of Sensoria) to his local Starbucks when Mario's wife spilled coffee on his foot and he felt that the heat burn through. The experience got Mario thinking that, rather than having technology attached to clothing, the textile itself needs to be the sensorial computer. After researching and testing, the Sensoria Fitness Socks were born.

"We knew there were textile materials on the market which tried to address this, but they tended to lose effectiveness once washed—which is obviously not ideal for a garment you exercise in! So we had to create our own textile sensor technology which is washable, but also very thin and comfortable," said Davide Vigano, the CEO of Sensoria.

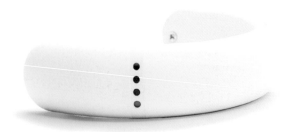

How It Works

The socks have sensors placed over the metatarsals on the right and the left and an additional sensor over the heel. These sensors communicate via an electronic, light anklet that users wear on one ankle. The companion app then lets runners know whether they are heel striking, over-striding or running at the wrong cadence. All of the data collected such as speed, distance, altitude gains, and GPS track are transmitted to the Sensoria Fitness app via the Bluetooth® anklet connected to the sock. Users will then get information such as cadence and running form in real time.

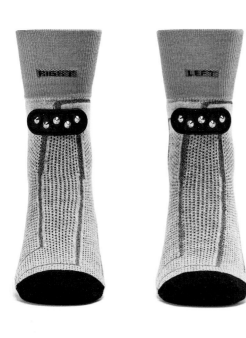

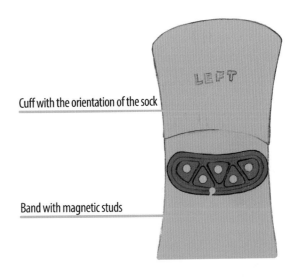

Cuff with the orientation of the sock

Band with magnetic studs

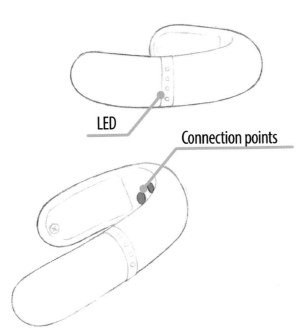

LED

Connection points

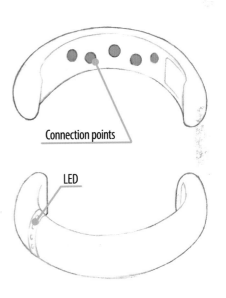

Connection points

LED

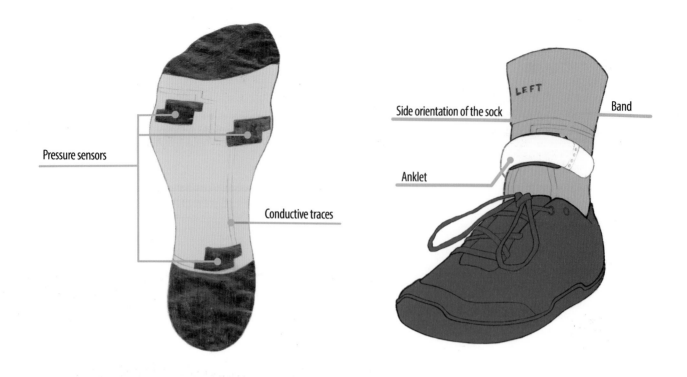

Pressure sensors

Conductive traces

Side orientation of the sock

Band

Anklet

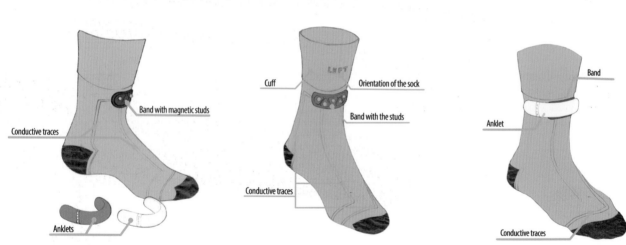

Band with magnetic studs

Conductive traces

Anklets

Cuff

Orientation of the sock

Band with the studs

Conductive traces

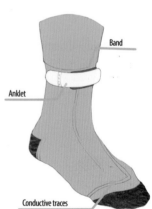

Band

Anklet

Conductive traces

How to Address

The anklet has flexible PCP electronics inside and can be bent and adjusted to various sizes of ankle sizes. You can just connect it and snap it through to the sock and stop to touch it after it's linked to the sock. It's magnetically connected to the sock. As soon as you connect it, it turns on. And as soon as you disconnect it, it turns off.

UP MOVE™

Co: Jawbone

UP MOVE™ is an activity tracker, a sleep tracker and it hooks you up to Smart Coach—a fitness app— with which UP MOVE™ teams up to make living a well-balanced life easier than ever. The small tracker is designed to be versatile, giving users flexibility in how to wear it.

UP4™

Co: Jawbone

UP4™ is a tracker that pays. It watches out for your health and fitness, all while making life a little more convenient. Imagine you're cooling down after a run and decide you want a smoothie— stop in, order and tap-to-pay with your UP4™ tracker. No fumbling around in pockets or wallets, simply link your UP4™ to your eligible American Express® Card and you're all set.

NOVA is a personal climbing wall that redefines training at home, making it a celebrated activity through a new take on design expression and a compelling interactive interface.

The wall consists of panels with pattern cut-outs, which replace the colored holds usually found on regular training walls. To offer a variety of climbing routes and difficulty levels, routes are flexibly indicated through light. Users select a route using their iPhone and receive personalized training. When not in use, Nova's lighting mode creates a modern ambience. Nova is a game-changing home training wall that supports a healthy lifestyle.

CURV

De: Samantha Jo Floersch

CURV is a revolutionary product that eliminates the need for headphones while biking. With a Bluetooth connection, the user can connect to their personal device while keeping track of the weather, heart rate, location and speed. CURV attaches to the back of a helmet to ensure its secure.

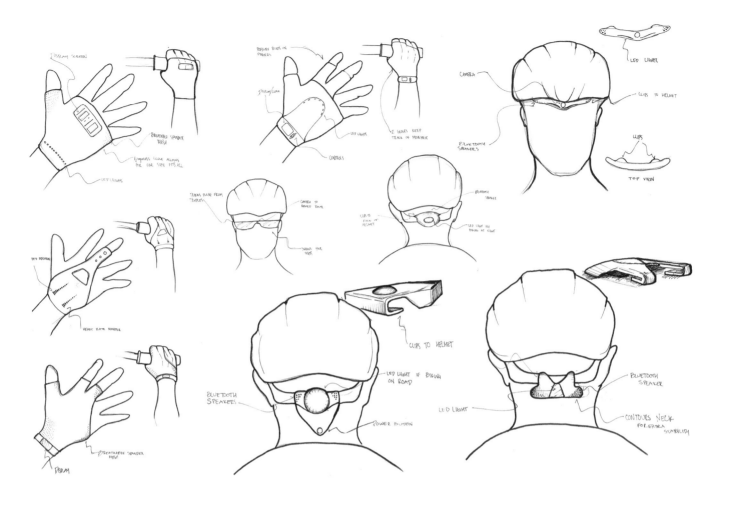

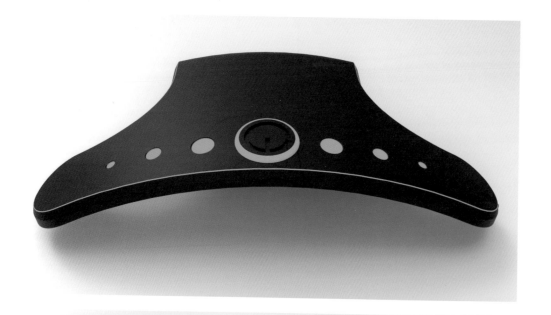

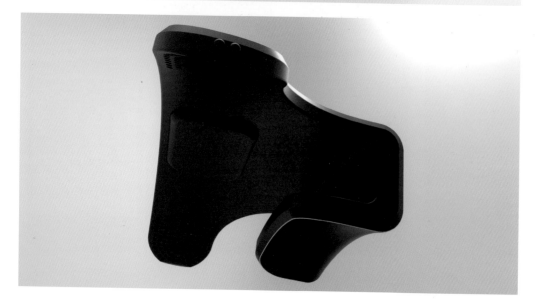

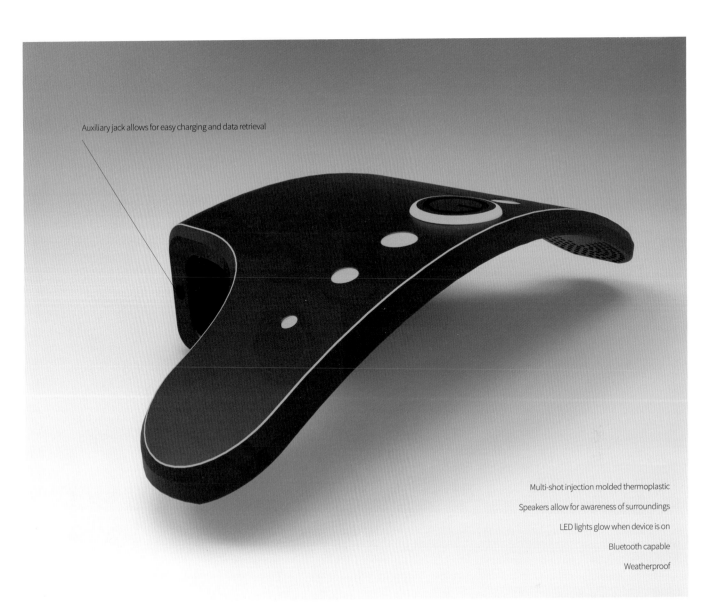

Auxiliary jack allows for easy charging and data retrieval

Multi-shot injection molded thermoplastic

Speakers allow for awareness of surroundings

LED lights glow when device is on

Bluetooth capable

Weatherproof

Volume buttons conveniently located

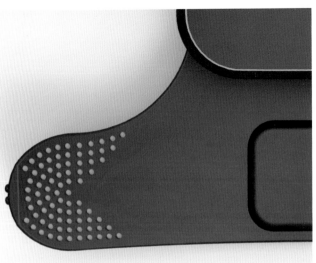

Heart rate monitor sits at base of neck

Intelligent Riding Monitor

De: Shenzhen AZ Industrial Design Co., Ltd

This intelligent riding monitor can show you all the data you need when you are riding, including speed, distance, and body data like pulse. It also connects to your cellphone; via its app, you can share your sport info with your friends, and create your personal sport plan and so on.

Sensoria Sports Bra and Fitness T-shirt

Co: Sensoria Fitness Inc.

The Sensoria sports bra and running T-shirt have heart rate sensors woven into them. Thanks to the sensors, the sports wearables provide accurate, consistent heart rate monitoring, and allow users to read the detected data such as steps, cadence, distance, GPS information, and calories burned through an accompanying app. Appropriate fabric makes them light and breathable: 74% polyamide, 18% polyester and 8% elastane for the bra while 95% polyamide and 5% elastance for the T-shirt. The fabric also removes humidity and allows users' body stay dry by virtue of Sensoria sweat wicking technology.

1. Wet the heart rate sensors.

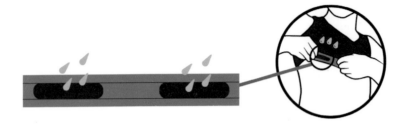

2. Attach your heart rate monitor to the snaps.

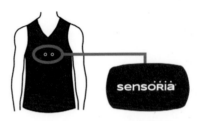

3. Make sure you have the sensors in direct contact with your skin.

Heart rate monitor

Heart rate monitor

152 BPM
HEART RATE

Sensoria Fitness T-shirt

62% BALL
FOOT LANDING

180 steps/min
CADENCE

Sensoria Fitness Socks

●●●●● AT&T 2:04 PM ✳ 100%

‹ Statistics Splits Map

8/4/15, 3:53 PM   29:10

153   377
HEART RATE ·   CALORIES
BPM   kCal

3.3   768
DISTANCE   ALTITUDE
miles   ft

90% BALL   378
FOOT LANDING   FOOT CONTACT
                  ms

170   8:50
CADENCE   PACE
steps/min   min/mile

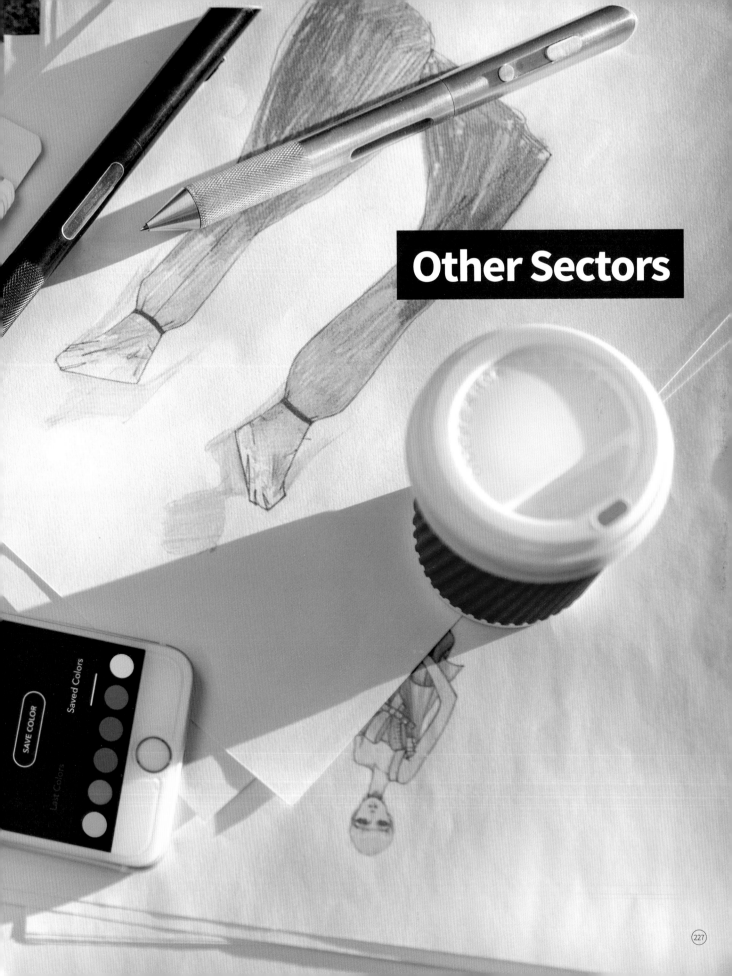

Other Sectors

Smart kapp

Co: SMART Technologies Inc.

The Smart kapp dry-erase board is a new device allowing people to share contents in real time and collaborate with others in a simple but powerful way. The board allows users to write, draw and capture ideas using any dry-erase marker, just like the old-fashioned dry-erase board, while enabling them to instantly save their work images, convert them to PDFs, and instantly send to anyone, anywhere. It is a tool designed to improve business productivity and collaboration. The product consists of two parts, the whiteboard itself and the accompanying app.

How the Board Story Begins?

The leaders of SMART Technologies saw a need for a new dry-erase board, a board easy to use—literally. People don't have to go through some training to learn how to use it. The only thing they need to do is to walk up and use. The team further developed the concept and aimed to make it 1) affordable; 2) simple to use as writing on a dry-erase board and smart; 3) mobile-friendly. This concept guided the product development and the team was finally paid back by a popular, user-friendly and mobile-device compatible board.

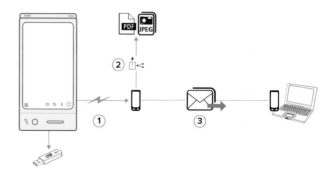

How the Board Works?

SMART kapp uses SMART's proprietary DViT® (Digital Vision Touch) technology: the four cameras and retroflective material of the board see bright bands. When there is a sudden dark spot, each camera detects them and figures out whether it's a finger, a pen or an eraser. Then it "draws" those dark spots—the writing—on the SMART kapp board to a mobile device, replicating what's written on the board.

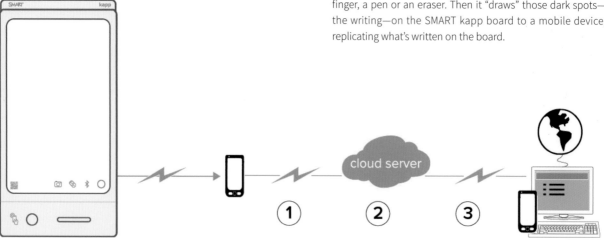

Simple to Use

To start the board, users just need to plug it in, download the app from the App Store and use the QR-code (or NFC/Board ID) to connect. As soon as the device is connected, the content on the Smart kapp will be updated live on users' mobile devices and can be shared in real time with anyone, no matter where they are. Users can also capture or save the content in JPEG or PDF format, in the cloud or to USB.

"I think the reason SMART kapp has been so well received is its simplicity and relevance in our everyday working lives. We all go to meetings. We all struggle with the challenge of involving remote attendees. One of the great things about SMART kapp is that it solves these challenges in an incredibly simple way. No one has time for extensive product training—with SMART kapp you simply hang it on the wall, scan the QR code with your phone and setup is complete. There's no need for training and that's critical for product adoption."

Appearance Design

The initial board mockup is glass-topped, a result that was untraditional and had the potential to be disruptive—there was nothing like those in SMART's portfolio at the time.

"The hardware features a truly innovative industrial design, making it a modern streamlined addition to any workspace. Our industrial designers worked hard on the appearance, wanting to ensure it would fit in at even the most modern workspaces. There are two variants of the hardware: the 42" model which is a glass whiteboard and the 84" model which is a steel version. Both feature a similar industrial design profile."

eHat

Co: Katapult Design Pty Ltd

The eHat system was conceived to allow inexperienced tradesman the opportunity to train on the job without the need for direct supervision. By utilizing eHat's video and voice connectivity, on-site tradesman can communicate with experienced supervisors remotely in real time, letting them see and hear what they are experiencing without actually being there. eHat is both a safety product and communications device.

Please introduce the technologies applied to eHat.

-HD camera to film the work area;
-High brightness LED lights for work area illumination;
-Communication indicator LED lights in the operator's peripheral vision;
-Built-in headset (earphones and microphone);
-Wi-Fi, Bluetooth and RF communication technologies;
-Approved safety helmet (hard hat);
-Smartphone app.

Did you meet any challenges when designing eHat?

Safety: One of the major challenges was that the eHat is both a safety product and communications device. It had to meet all the typical design requirements of an industrial hard hat, as well as include a broad array of electronics equipment.

Balance: The design and layout of the internal components needed to be well balanced so that eHat was both comfortable and balanced on the head for long periods of use.

Communications: Getting the eHat to perform complex communications in real time has been a real challenge. Our electronics team has worked tirelessly with service providers to ensure the system doesn't have any communication lag.

How did you balance the market feedback and the concept expression?

eHat has had several rounds of prototyping, including an appearance model and a fully functioning model. The prototypes have been used for both internal reviews and industry presentations and have allowed us the opportunity to get great feedback on the design and also create interest in the product.

We went to great lengths to ensure that the prototypes were highly representative of the finished design.

Your team has completed a batch of good products. What do you think is the most important aspect of the design job?

For us, user-centered design is the key. We're always championing their needs and putting them first in decision making. That said, it becomes a delicate balancing act between absolute design freedom and pragmatic commercial and manufacturing needs.

By maintaining a deep attention to detail and continuously questioning the status quo, we aim to create products that have a positive effect on their intended ecosystem.

Often, to do this our designers need to think beyond what is expected and approach problems from different angles. It is also absolutely crucial that we work as a team, not only within Katapult, but with our clients and industry partners. It is always very rewarding to see like-minded creatives solve tricky problems in a way that provides that level of surprise and delight that was never anticipated.

LED stripe

SPEAKERS
IN RIM.

1 TOP CASE.
  LENS/SHELL

2 MAIN BODY

GLOWS
RED?

3 INNER
  TECH
  (SOFT)

MIRROR.
LED
LENS.

FRONT LENS
CAMERA.

INNER LENS
(HIDES CAMERA)

EAR
MUFFS.

IN BUILT
SPEAKER.

CAMERA INDICATOR
(RECESSED)

UNDERSIDE
DETAIL.

LENS DROPS.

SLIGHTLY
RECESSED.

REAR
DETAIL.

IN BUILT
MIC PORT.

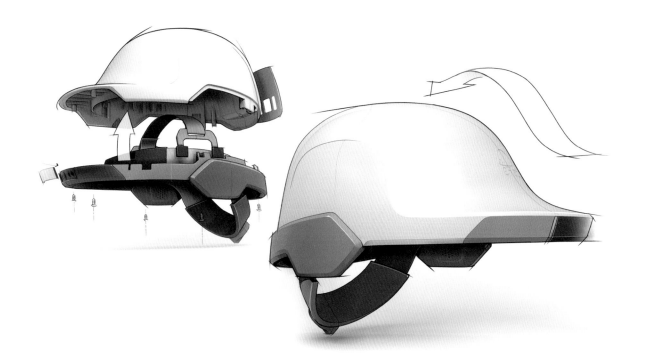

Cronzy Pen

Co: Cronzy Inc.

The Cronzy Pen is a handheld, high-tech art tool that allows you to write and draw in whatever color you like. With the most extensive selection of built-in colors available on the market and the ability to scan and save any color from any object, the Cronzy Pen and its partner app helps artists to capture and reproduce every shade imaginable, and carry them all in a single, portable art tool. The Cronzy Pen's range of tip diameters allows its users to paint, draw, and write on everything from canvas to skin, and in variable widths too.

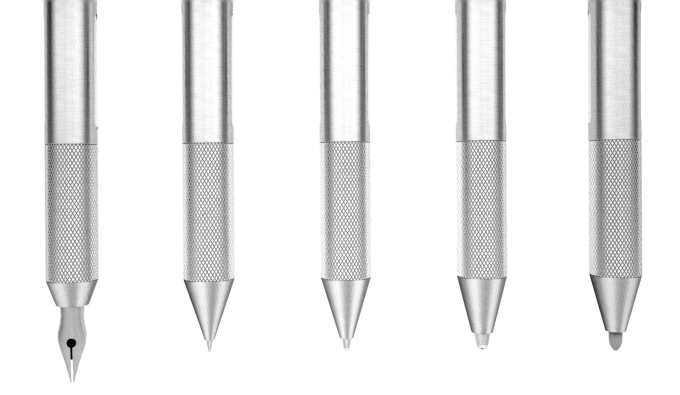

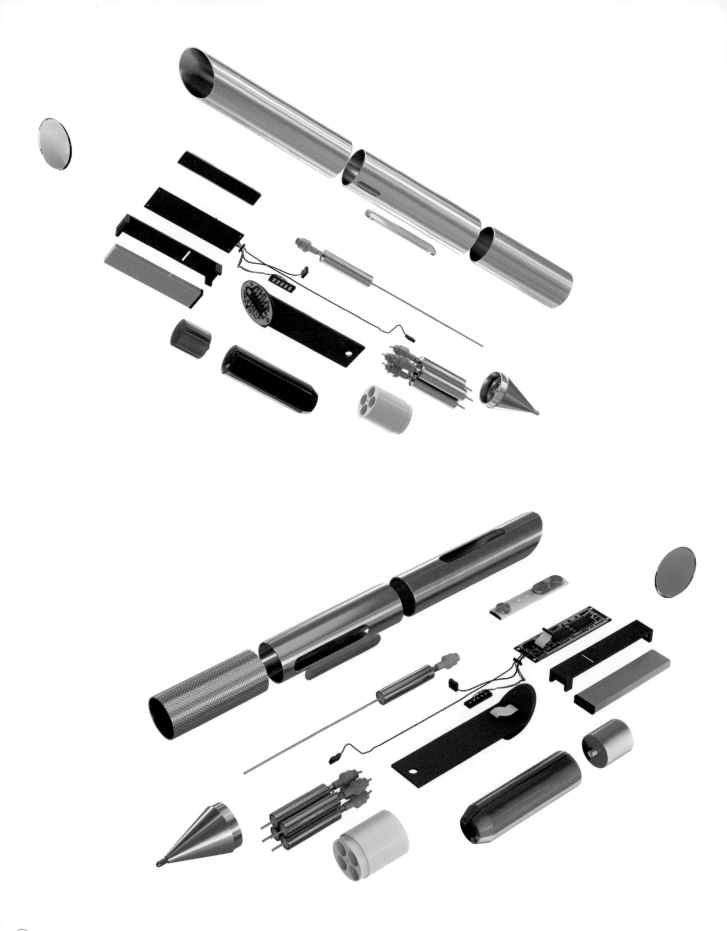

The Slate

Co: iskn

The Slate is a smart drawing pad for all creatives. It combines the unique and irreplaceable experience of drawing on paper with the limitless possibilities of digital. When users draw with their own pen or pencil on real paper, the action is enhanced with a magnetic ring. And 32 sensors spread across the Slate detect the ring and infer the position of the pen. The Slate then generates a graphic render, and the drawing comes to life in real time on the user's screen (on iPad, iPhone, Mac or PC).

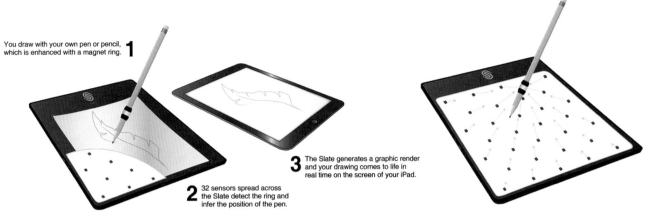

You draw with your own pen or pencil, which is enhanced with a magnet ring. **1**

3 The Slate generates a graphic render and your drawing comes to life in real time on the screen of your iPad.

2 32 sensors spread across the Slate detect the ring and infer the position of the pen.

32 magnometers track the position, orientation, and tilt angle of the ring in 3D space (X,Y,Z) with high precison.

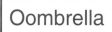

Oombrella

Co: Wezzoo

Oombrella is a smart, connected umbrella that alerts you before it rains and if you leave it behind. What makes the umbrella smart is the handle, which is the "brain" of the device. It contains four sensors to respectively detect temperature, pressure, humidity and light, and talks to your smartphone using the Bluetooth Low Energy technology. Behind these functions is the platform Wezzoo, a social and real-time weather service. Users can share the weather information they experience with the community, making hyperlocal weather data more accurate.

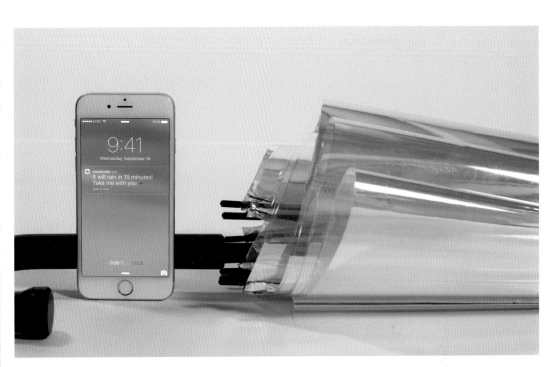

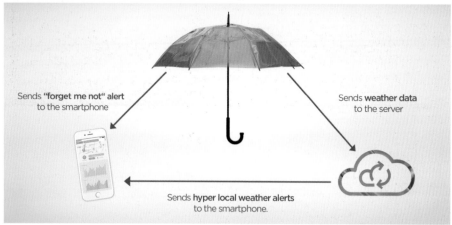

Sends **"forget me not"** alert to the smartphone

Sends **weather data** to the server

Sends **hyper local weather alerts** to the smartphone.

Kiddo Easy Parents System

De: Razy2 Design Group, Blast Lab, Many Colors

Consisting of a localization device, elastic changeable band and a charger, Kiddo is a system to help you to keep an eye on your children. When you and your kid wear Kiddo, the devices communicate with each other without a smartphone and vibrate when your child walks far away from you.

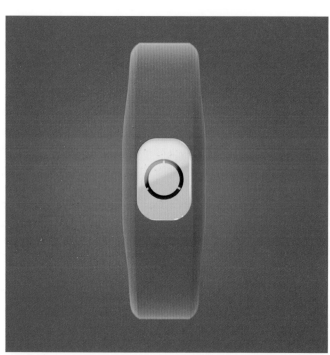

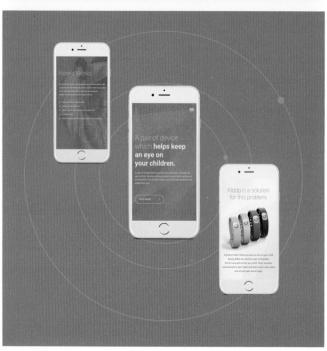

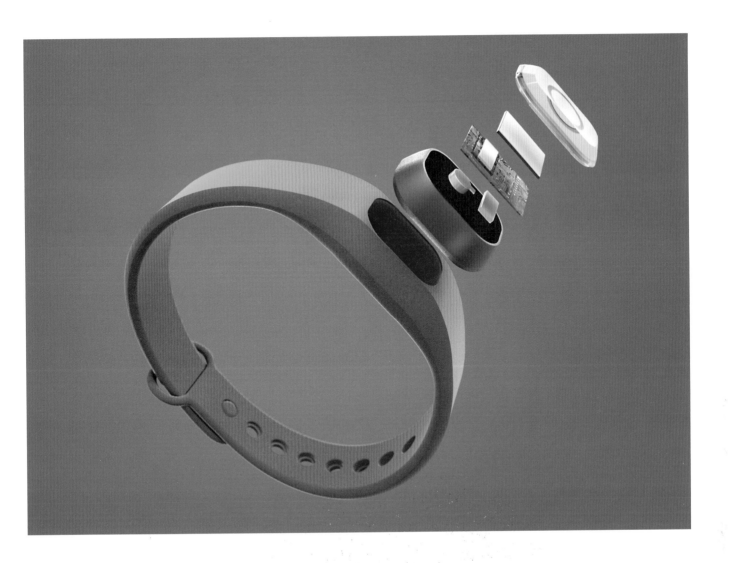

The devices were designed in a manner that children cannot remove them easily from their hands. It is unisex, attractive both to adults and young users. Since the elements are as small as technology permits, the devices look simple with nothing to be removed.

The Myo Armband

Co: Thalmic Labs

The Myo gesture and motion control armband lets you use the movements of your hands to effortlessly control your phone, computer, and so on. The Myo armband senses gesture and motion control to seamlessly interpret what your hands and fingers are doing, and transmits that information over Bluetooth to communicate with your favorite digital devices. Your movements and gestures are tracked in two ways: motions are detected by a nine-axis inertial measurement unit and gestures by proprietary electromyography sensors.

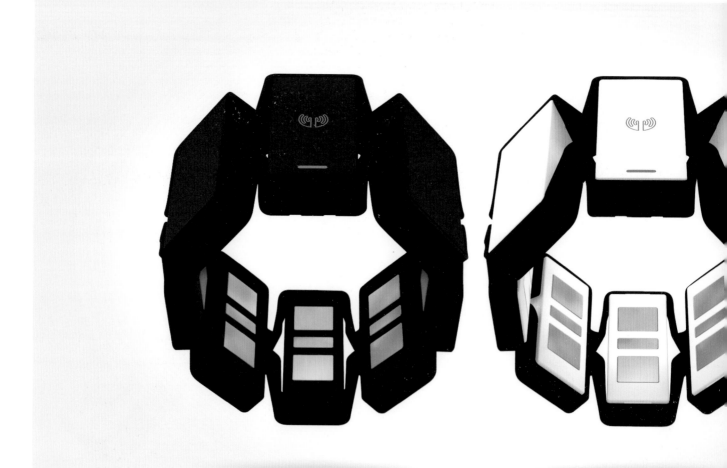

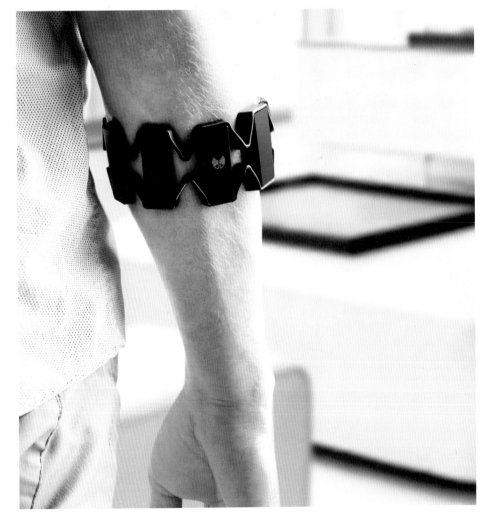

BLŌCKS

BLOCKS

Co: BLOCKS Wearables Inc

BLOCKS is a smartwatch that is built with a modular band. It breaks away from the size-related compromise that faces many smartwatches on the market. Smartwatch makers typically have to limit their choice of features. The BLOCKS strap is made up of different modules, each built with a specialized sensor or feature so that wearers can build a device that's unique to them. All modules are "plug-n-play" such that users can quickly and effortlessly swap in features. Currently available features include: Heart Rate, GPS, LED, Environmental sensors and Extra Battery modules. In future, BLOCKS aim to release a Sim Card module, Biometric Fingerprint Identification, NFC contactless payments, a Camera, and more. The BLOCKS device provides freedom of choice for consumers and brings customization to the hardware world.

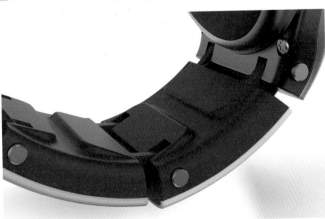

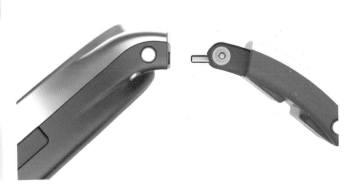

Mobispot

De: Katerina Kopytina

Mobispot is a project all about connecting digital applications and people's everyday life. It creates wearable NFC devices for daily use. With three wearable options, users can do everything from buying transport ticket to making micro-payments, to accessing control/campus functions, securing identification and saving loyalty and member-ship cards, etc.

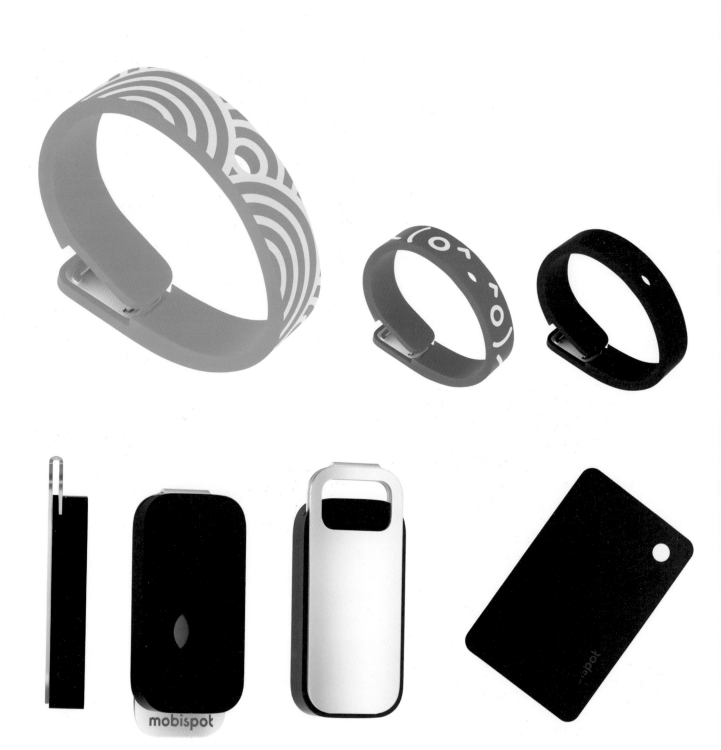

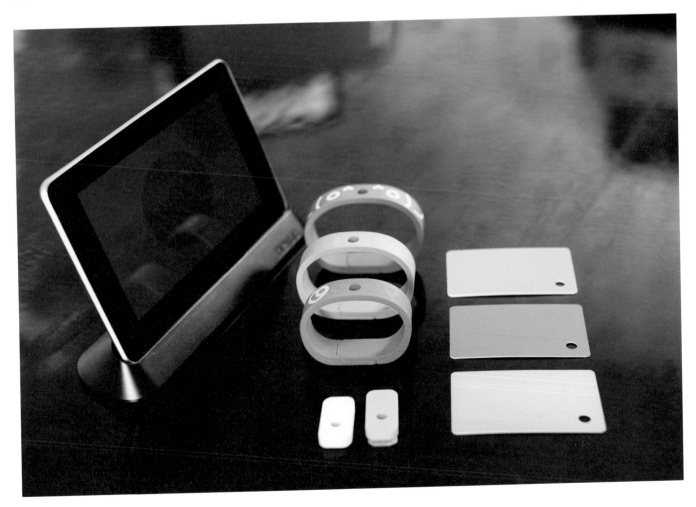

De: Franka Isabella Bellinda

ARVI-E (short for Autism Robot Assistant with Visual Intelligence - Educational Features) is an interactive device conceived for children with ASD for their preparation in facing society, helping them to develop life skills. The functions are to stimulate their senses; to develop motor skill; to develop them in social interaction; and to be the assistant for the parents to educate their children at home. To fulfill this aim, ARVI-E is equipped with Artificial Intelligence, Authorized Finger Print Button for activation, Mood Identification, Face Recognition and Bump Sensor (ultrasonic), Hologram Projector, and LED Pixel Display. The Hologram Projector, for example, allows parents to be shown when the children need their presence. Mood Identification detect children's mood and shows the mood by different colors and facial expressions, letting ASD children imitate expressions.

SKETCHES

THUMBNAIL & IDEA EXPLORATIONS

FINAL DESIGN

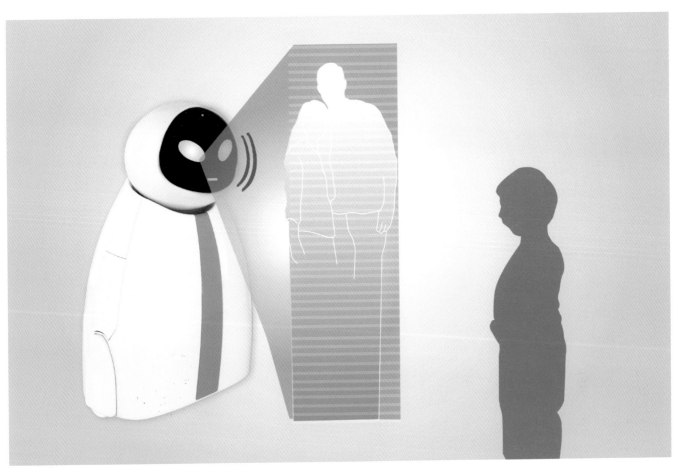

10 : 5 = 2

Co: AKA Intelligence

Musio is a robot powered by the A.I. engine "MUSE," which understands textual language, oral language, gestures, and facial expressions of human beings. With Muse, Musio can learn a human being's communication language and context, which makes possible the interaction and conversation with human beings. Musio has two product lines, one of which aims to be an English education tool for children of non-English speaking countries, like China, Japan, and Korea, etc.

Bluesmart One

Co: Bluesmart

Bluesmart One is a smart, connected carry-on suitcase. With intelligence injected, it allows users to check the bag's location from their smartphone and charge their devices. When the bag is left behind, it will lock itself. Users can check the weight of their bag right on their phone to avoid fees as well.

258

HiSmart
The First Smart, Convertible Urban Bag

Co: Lepow

HiSmart is a smart bag incorporating a batch of functions powered by HiRemote for a more efficient and enjoyable urban life. The specially designed HiRemote syncs with the HiSmart app. The 2-in-1 customized chip inside the strap enables users to pin locations, find HiSmart or a phone, answer calls, listen to music, record voice, and take selfies in just seconds.

HiSmart has clean lines and is suited for different occasions with its minimal embellishments. With a special German-designed Fidlock, it can change from a backpack to a messenger bag. By changing the orientation, the carrying capacity changes.

SELFIES
ARE SIMPLE

PLAY MUSIC
ANYWHERE

PUSH ONCE
TO RECORD

NEVER MISS
ANOTHER CALL

BUDDY SYSTEM

HiSmart finds smartphone.
Smartphone finds HiSmart.

ONE SECOND
TO PIN YOUR LOCATION

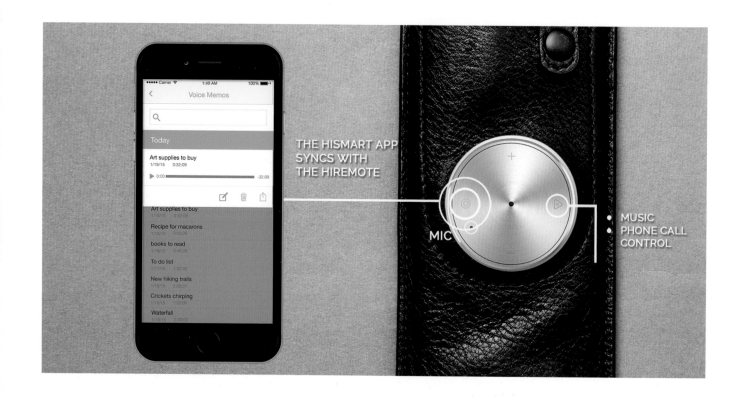

THE HISMART APP
SYNCS WITH
THE HIREMOTE

MIC

MUSIC
PHONE CALL
CONTROL

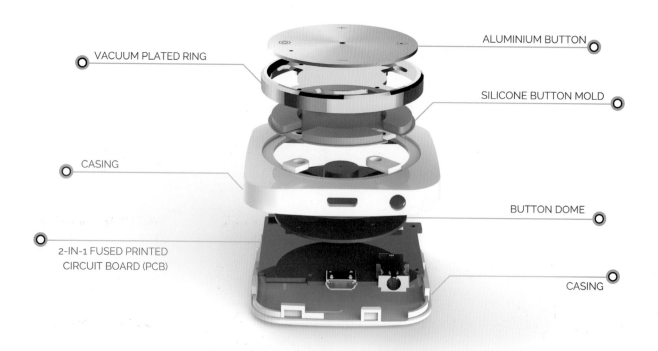

VACUUM PLATED RING

CASING

2-IN-1 FUSED PRINTED
CIRCUIT BOARD (PCB)

ALUMINIUM BUTTON

SILICONE BUTTON MOLD

BUTTON DOME

CASING

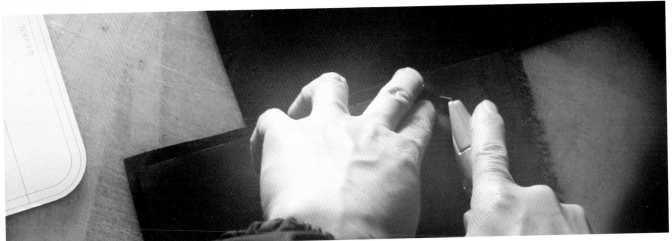

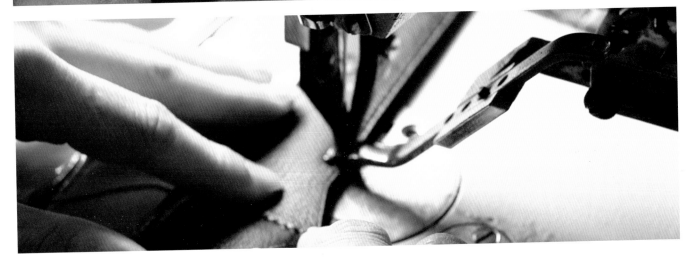

Pechat

Co: Hakuhodo Inc.

Pechat is a button-shaped speaker that can be attached a Teddy bear and gives it the power to talk. Controlled by a dedicated app, Pechat can be used in four modes: 1) voice chat: converts what the user says to a cute-sounding voice; 2) text chat: reads out input text in a cute-sounding voice using a high-quality voice-synthesis engine; 3) tap chat: lets you play prerecorded phrases, songs, and stories by selecting them on the screen; 4) auto chat: automatically responds to or mimics what your child says. That's to say, parents are able to share secrets with children, sing songs together, suggest their children take a nap, and read them a story, etc. It is a smart tool for parenting and a next-generation toy for children.

Solo

Co: Uniform

Powered by a human AI, Solo is a device that combines facial feature recognition with music valence to read the nuance of expression and match tracks to users' current mood. Solo starts by taking their photo as they approach. It then sends that photo to a Microsoft API that analyses features and sends that information back again as an emotional breakdown: values for happiness, sadness and anger. Solo translates these figures into a valence rating that corresponds with Spotify's track valence ratings. Then Solo plays the track it thinks its users want to hear most. It is kind of like a mix CD from a friend with great taste.

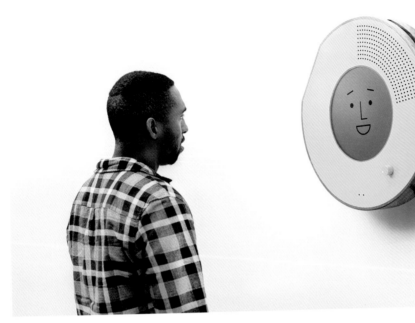

Voice Bridge

Co: invoxia

Voice Bridge is a smart gadget to give users more freedom when using communication tools. It allows users' cellphones to receive all incoming calls and place outgoing landline calls from anywhere. All incoming landline calls will ring on both users' landline and mobile, allowing them to take landline calls on the go. The device also allows connecting up to five mobile devices for a conference.

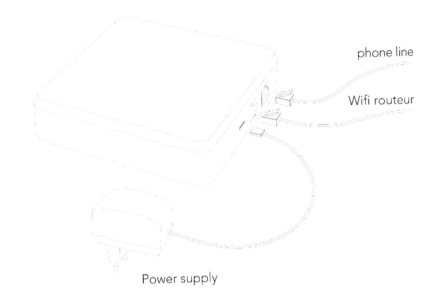

phone line

Wifi routeur

Power supply

INDEX

ACKNOWLEDGEMENTS

We would like to thank all the designers and contributors who have been involved in the production of this book; their contributions have been indispensable to its creation. We would also like to express our gratitude to all the producers for their invaluable opinions and assistance throughout this project. And to the many others whose names are not credited but have made helpful suggestions, we thank you for your continuous support.

FUTURE PARTNERSHIPS

If you wish to participate in SendPoints' future projects and publications, please send your website or portfolio to editor01@sendpoints.cn.